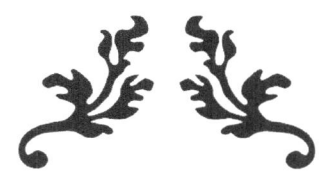

FLOWER MANDALAS & NATURE FOR ADULTS

THE BEST BOOK OF RELAXATION

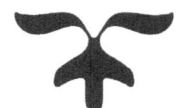

2020

GLADYS VALENCIA

Presentation

This beautiful coloring book was designed for all adults who want to leave behind anxiety, stress, worries, limiting thoughts, that exhaust us daily and do not allow us to be in a calm state of consciousness.

For this I invite you to take this book as your best ally. Set aside a moment of the day for yourself and enjoy filling with color and life each drawing thought of the flowers of a garden, animals and nature.

In this book you will find the best flower and animal nature mandalas, which with basic shapes will lead you to relax and free yourself from everyday anxiety. I recommend you accompany it with soft instrumental music and the soft aroma of a candle.

Enjoy its content!
Mrs. Gladys Valencia

The life you deserve to live.

The best tips and digital resources that I recommend to improve your quality of life and well-being.

Foolw us !!

Facebook: www.facebook.com/romeo101.hack.your.life

Instagram: @romeo101.hack.your.life

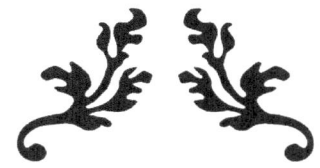

POSITIVE AFFIRMATIONS

Today is another beautiful day on Earth and we are going to live it with joy.

I surround myself with harmony and love for my family, my home, my friends and myself.

I walk away from any idea that hurts me, whatever the way I do it, even when it comes from those I love.

I go beyond the limitations of my loved ones, towards a new sense of freedom for me.

I no longer impose my old limitations on others: They are free to be themselves.

I give others what I want to receive.

Love and acceptance flow freely between my being and all the people I know.

We are one with the power that created us.

We are safe and secure, and all is well in our world.

That's right. Thank you Beloved Universe.

From the Author: Louise Hay

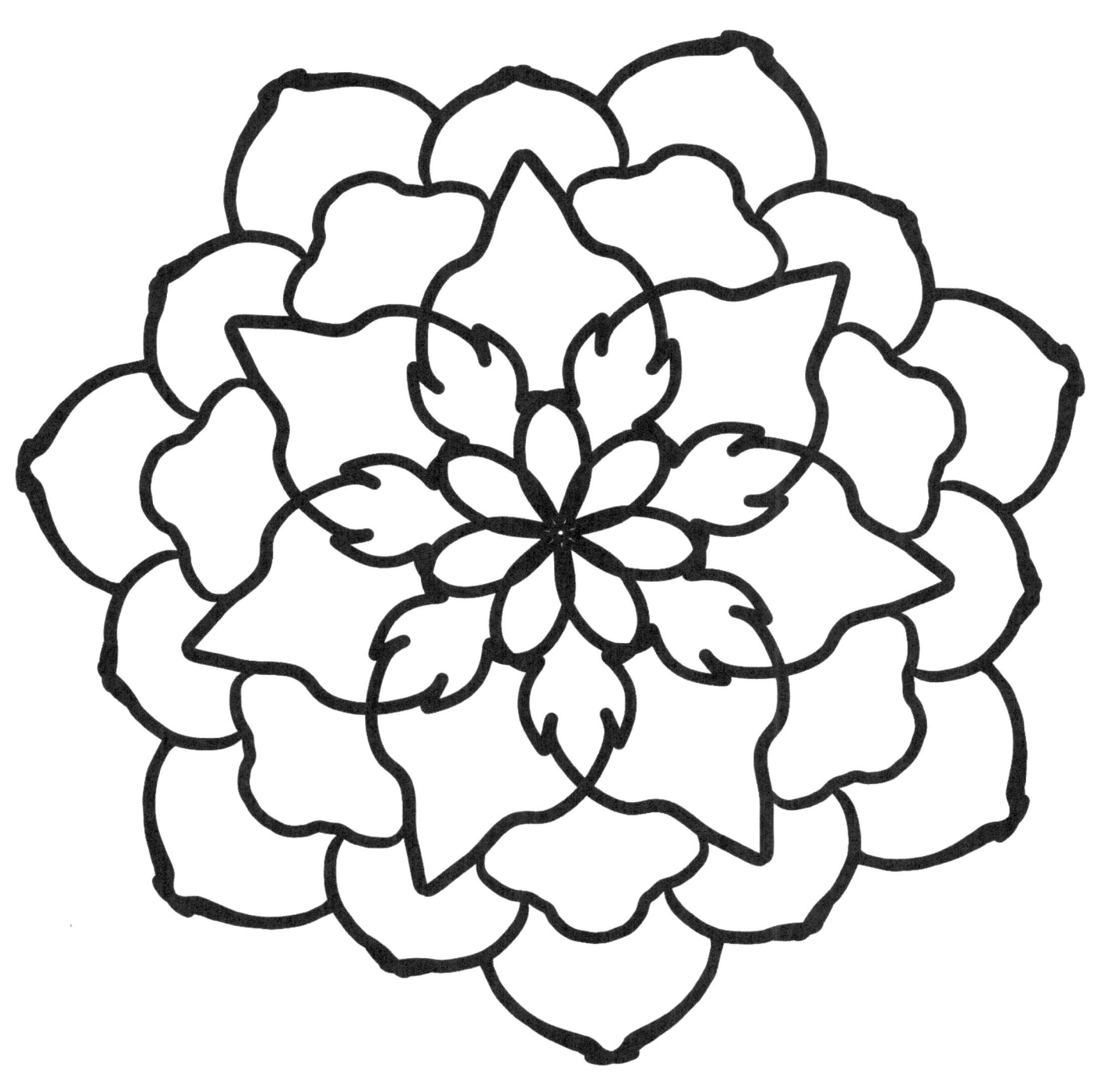

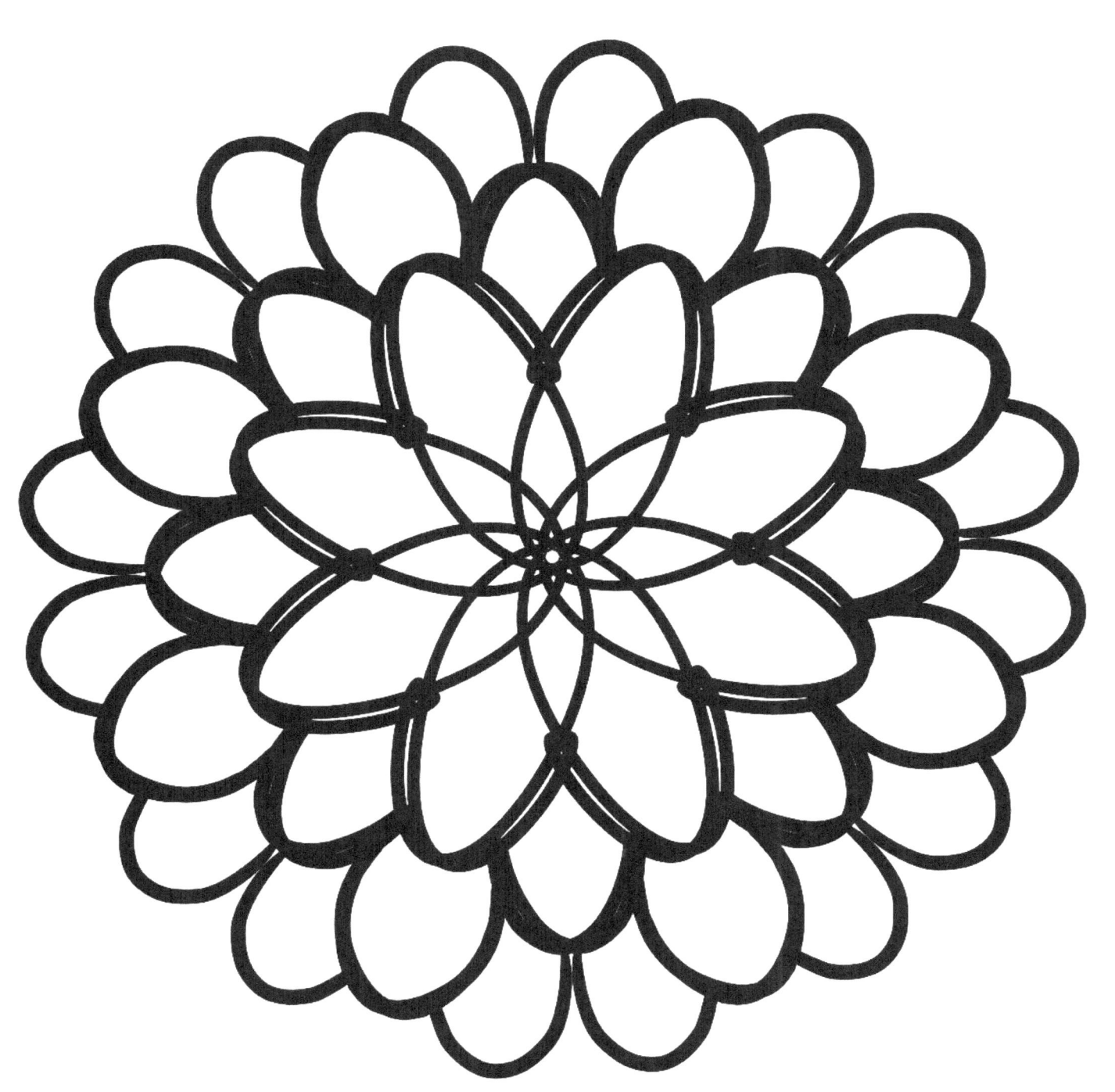

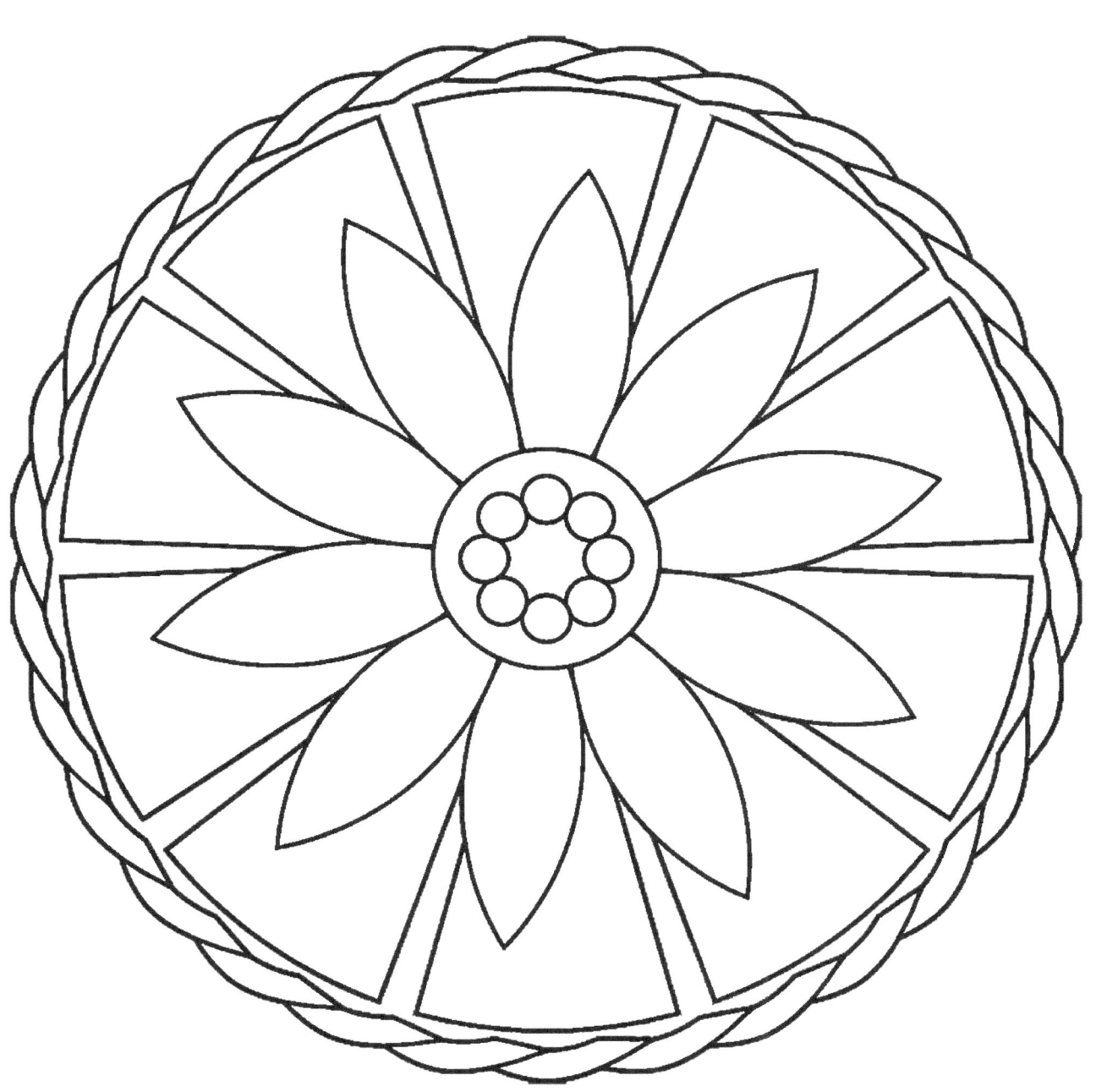

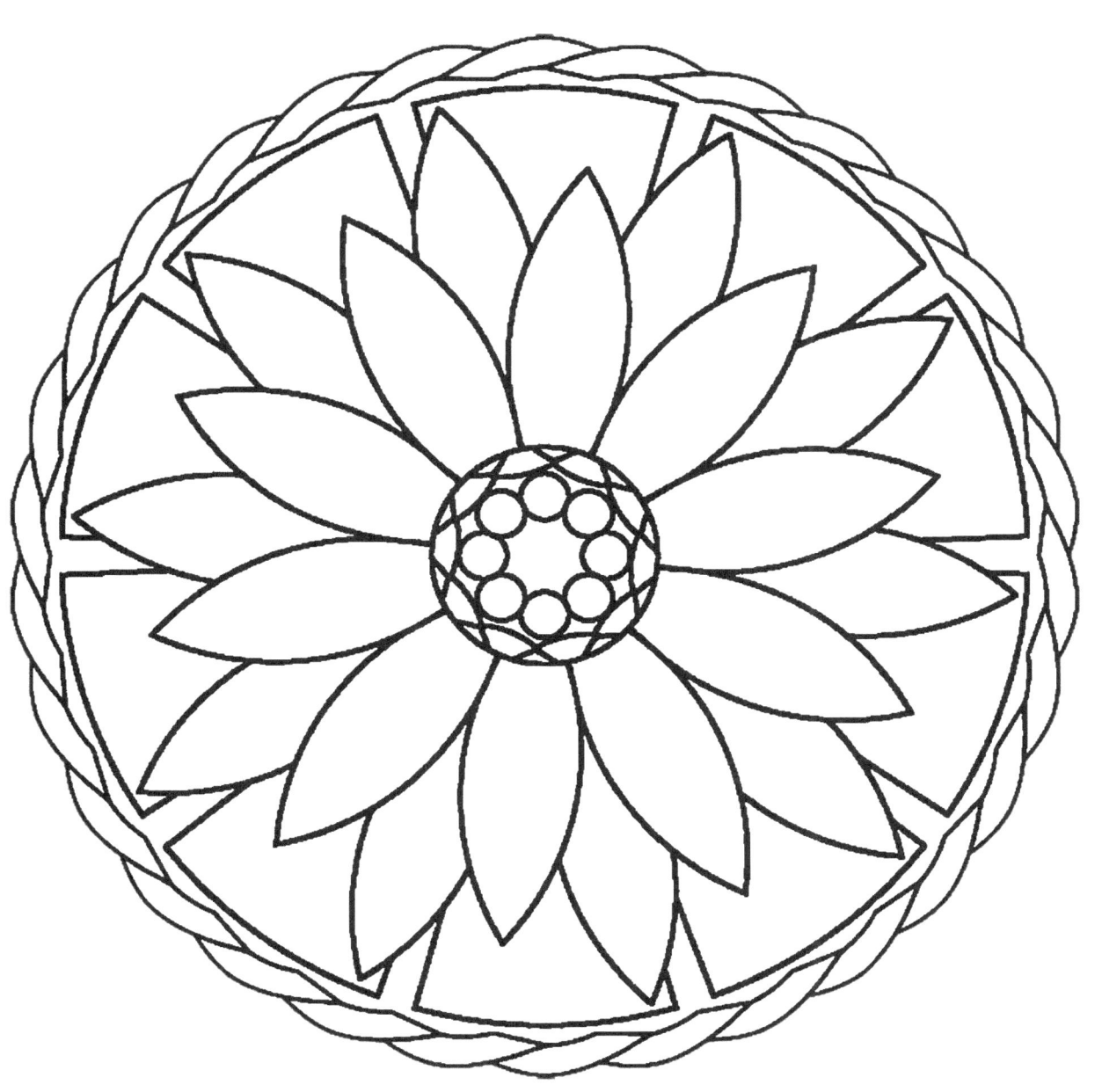

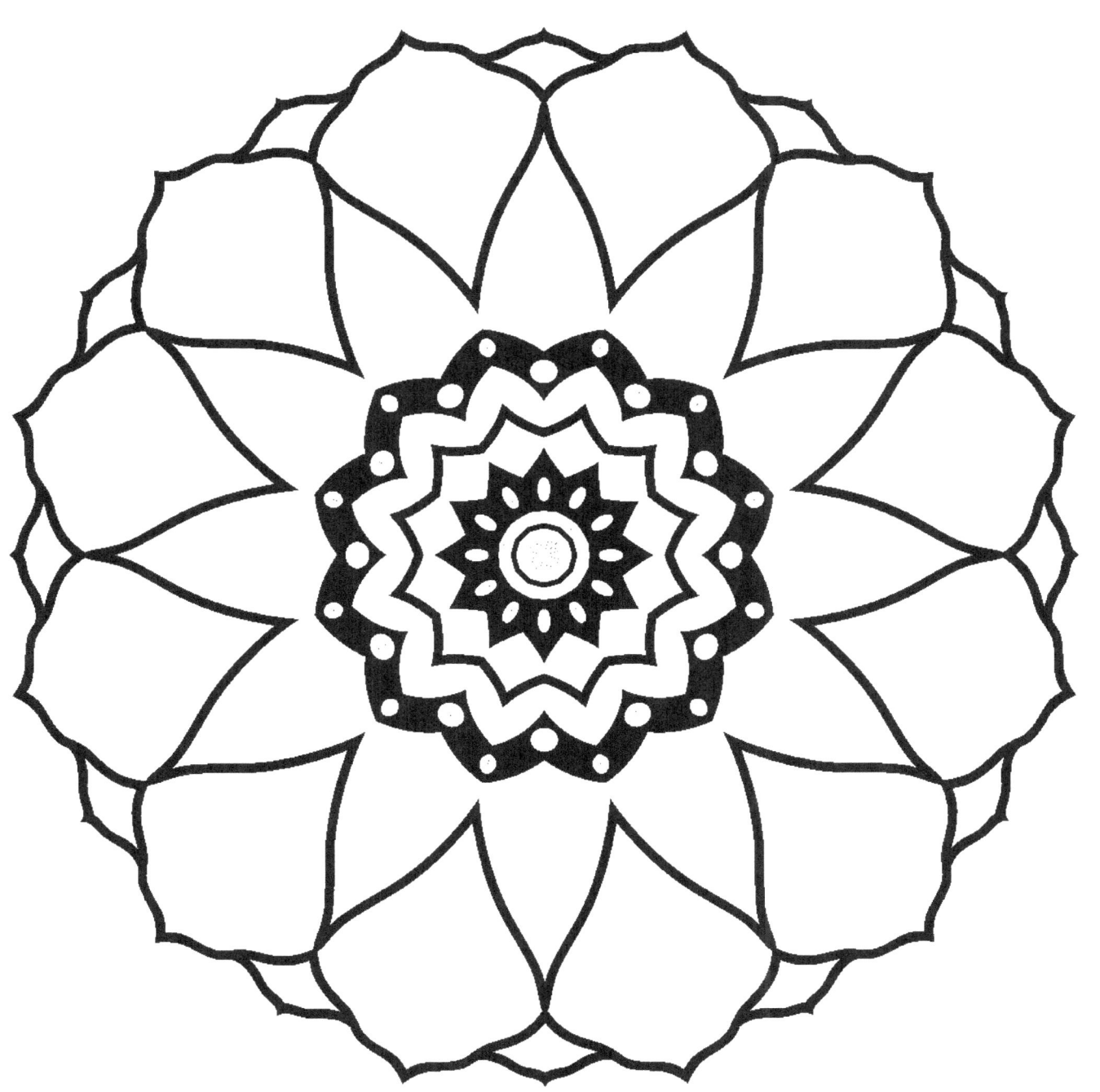

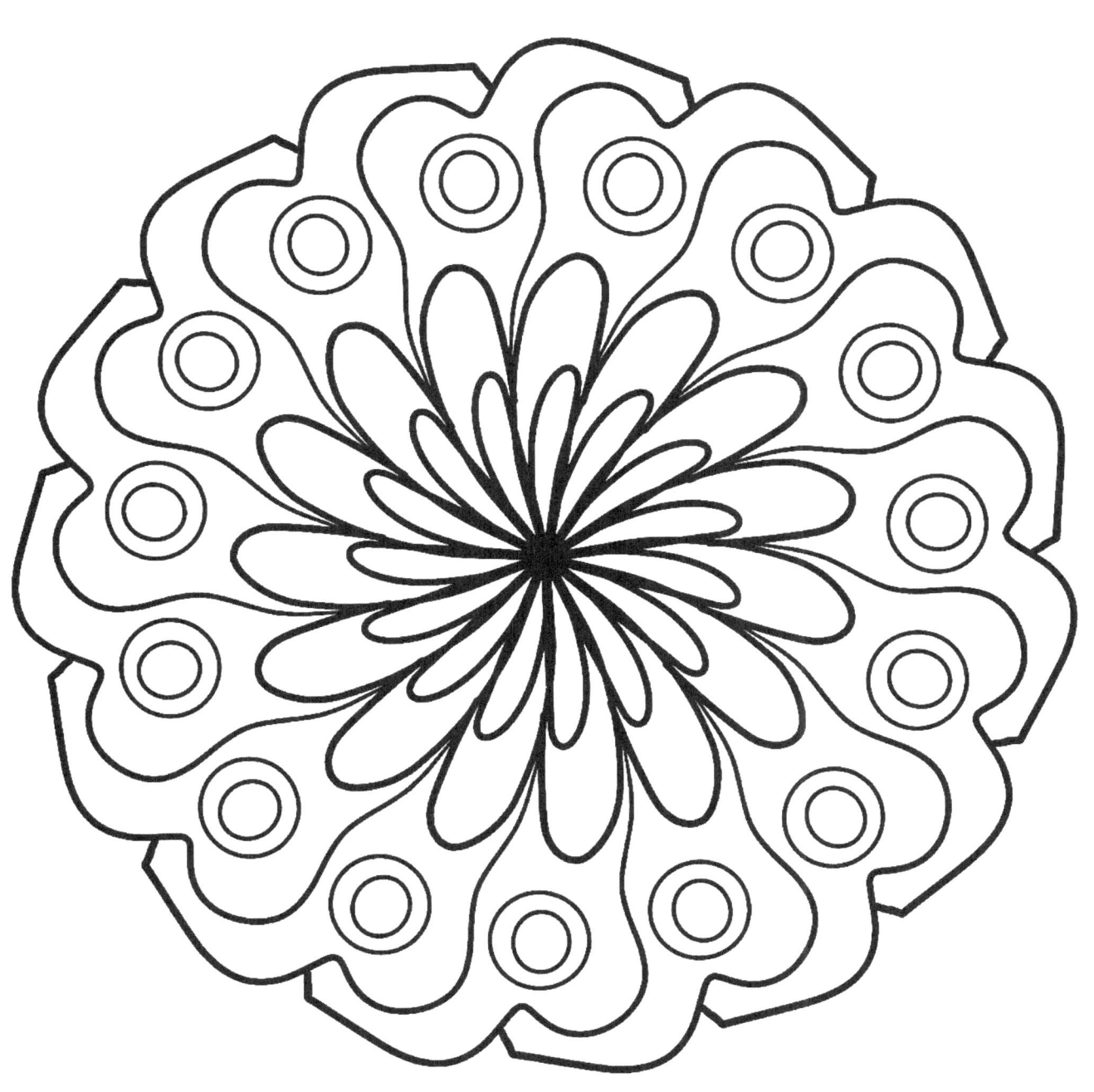

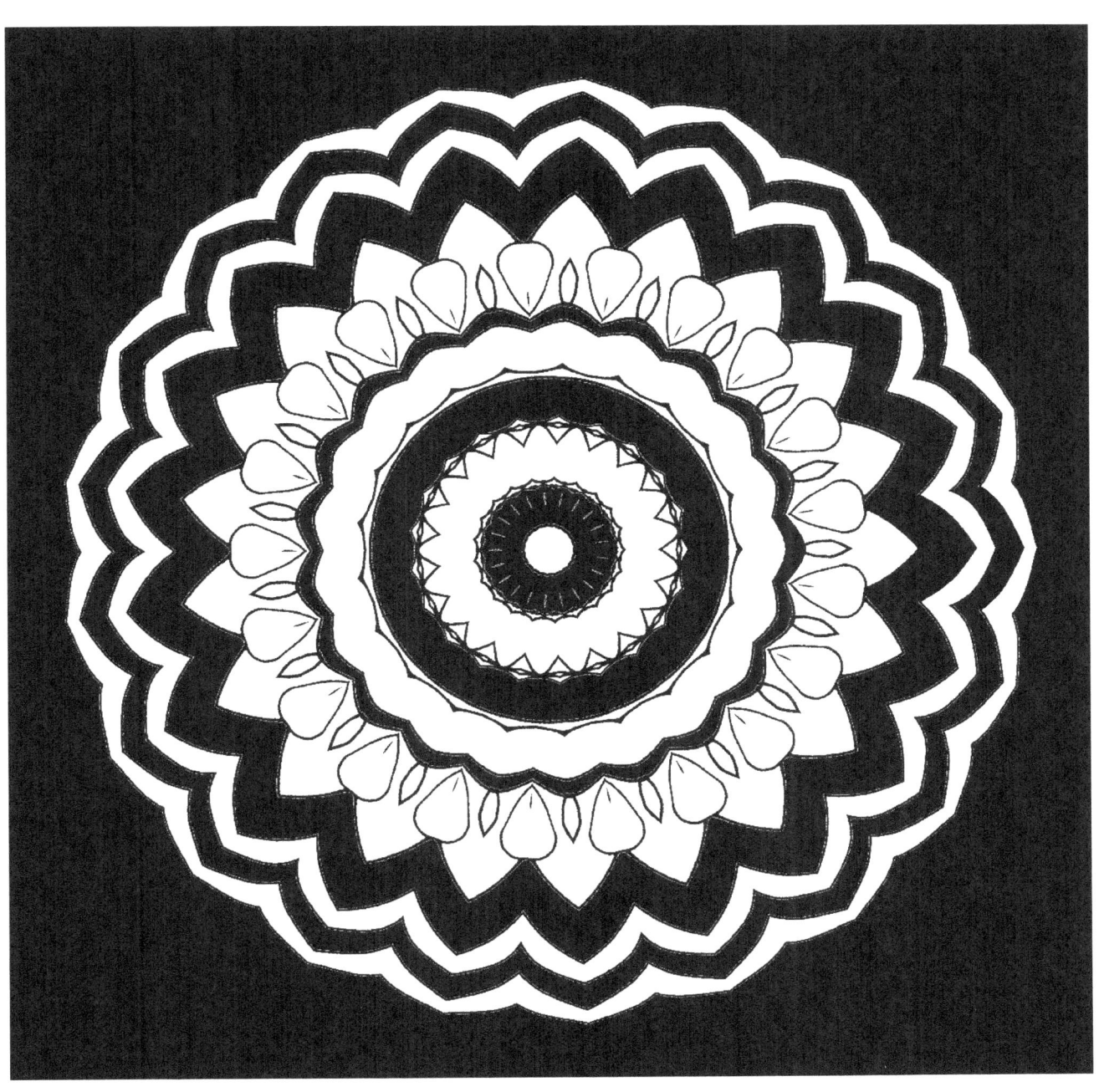

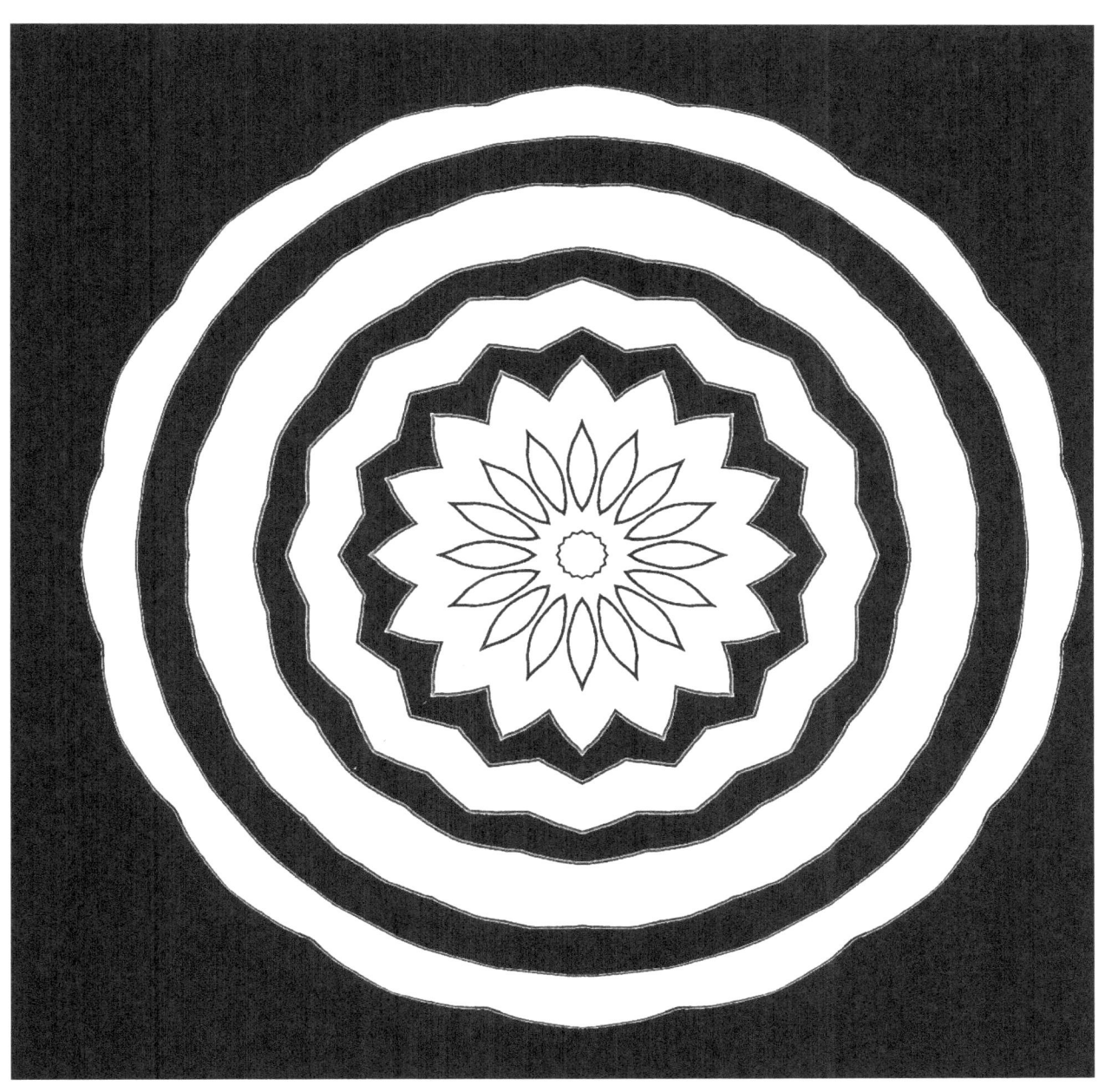

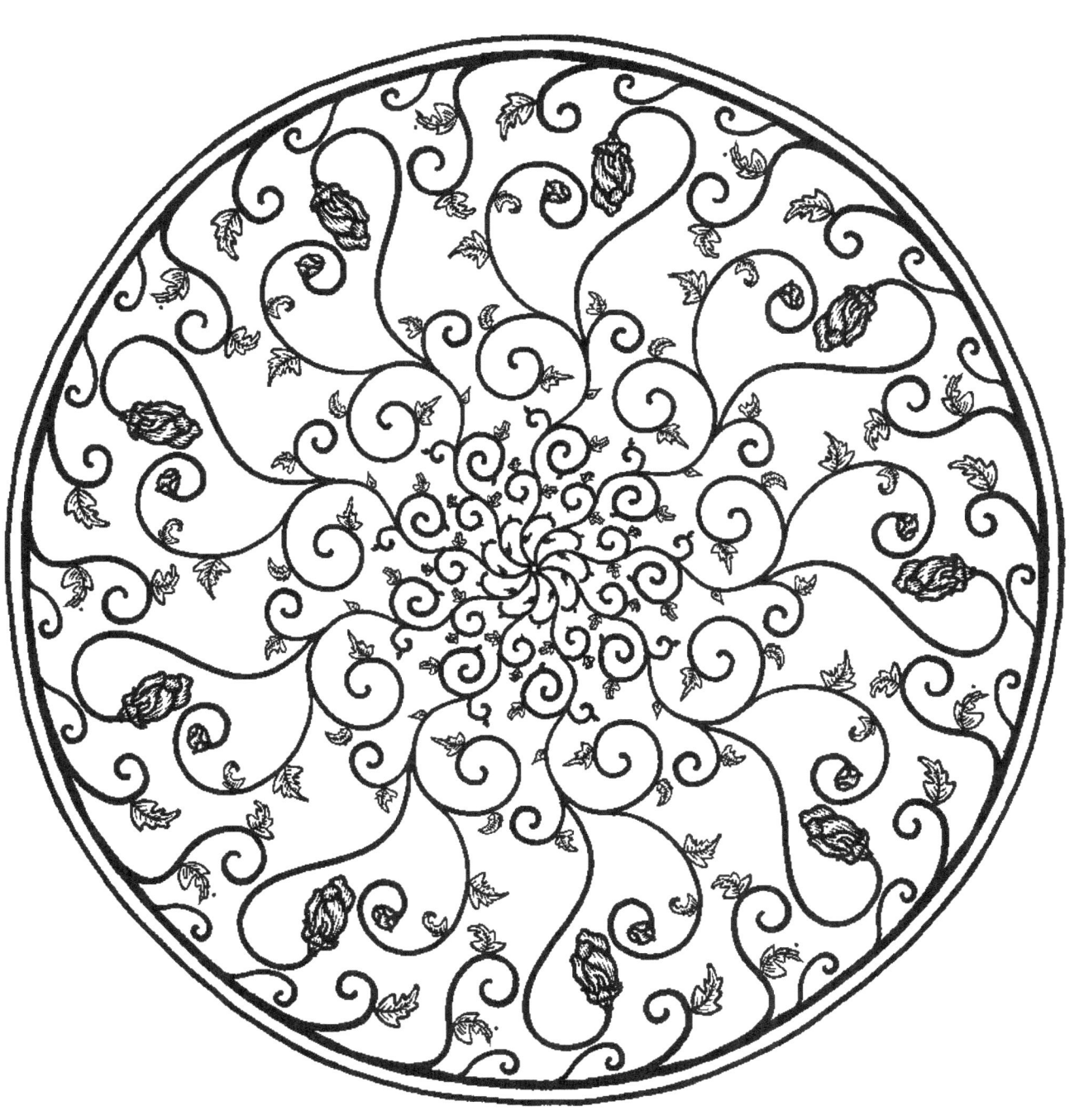

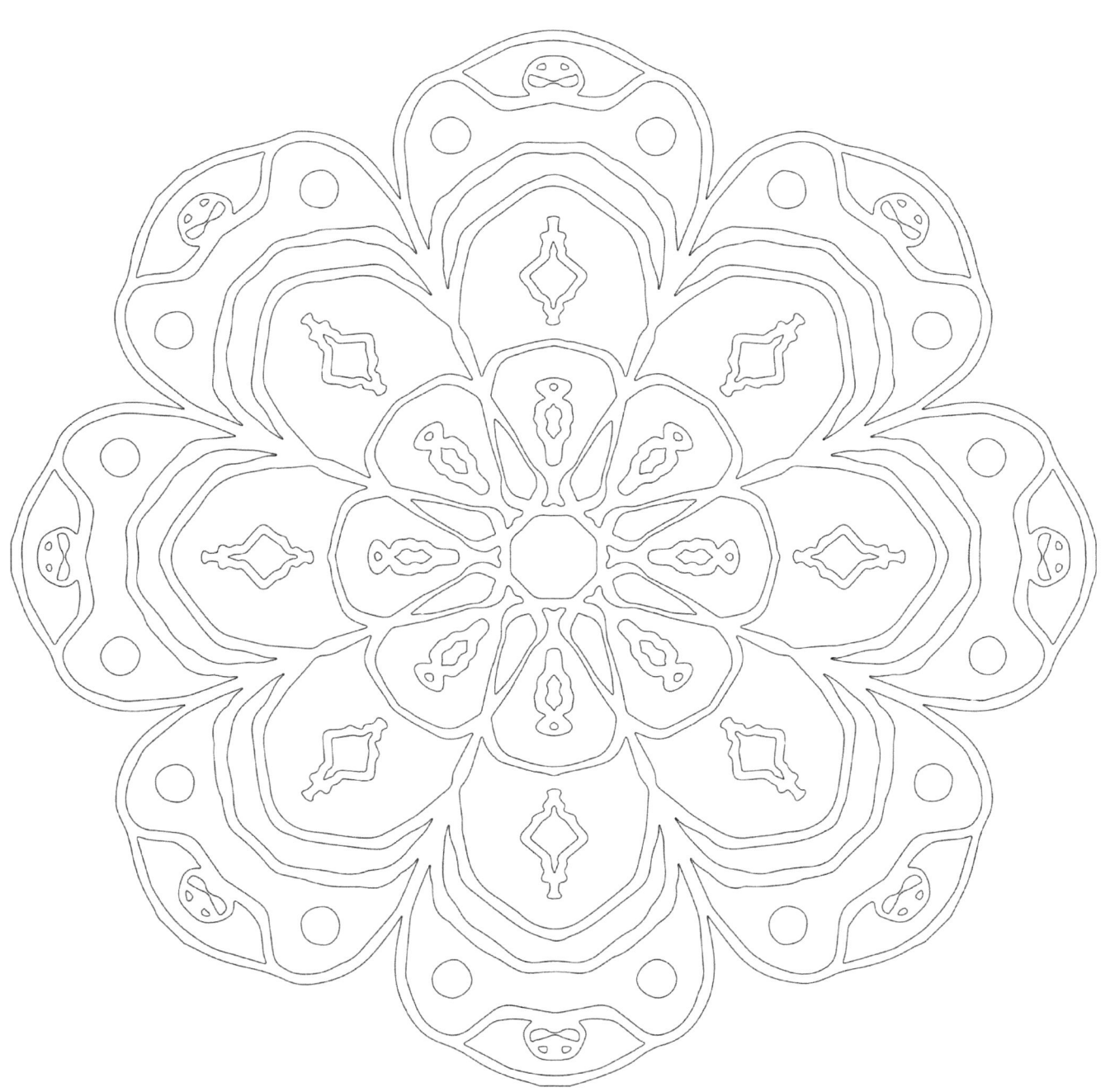

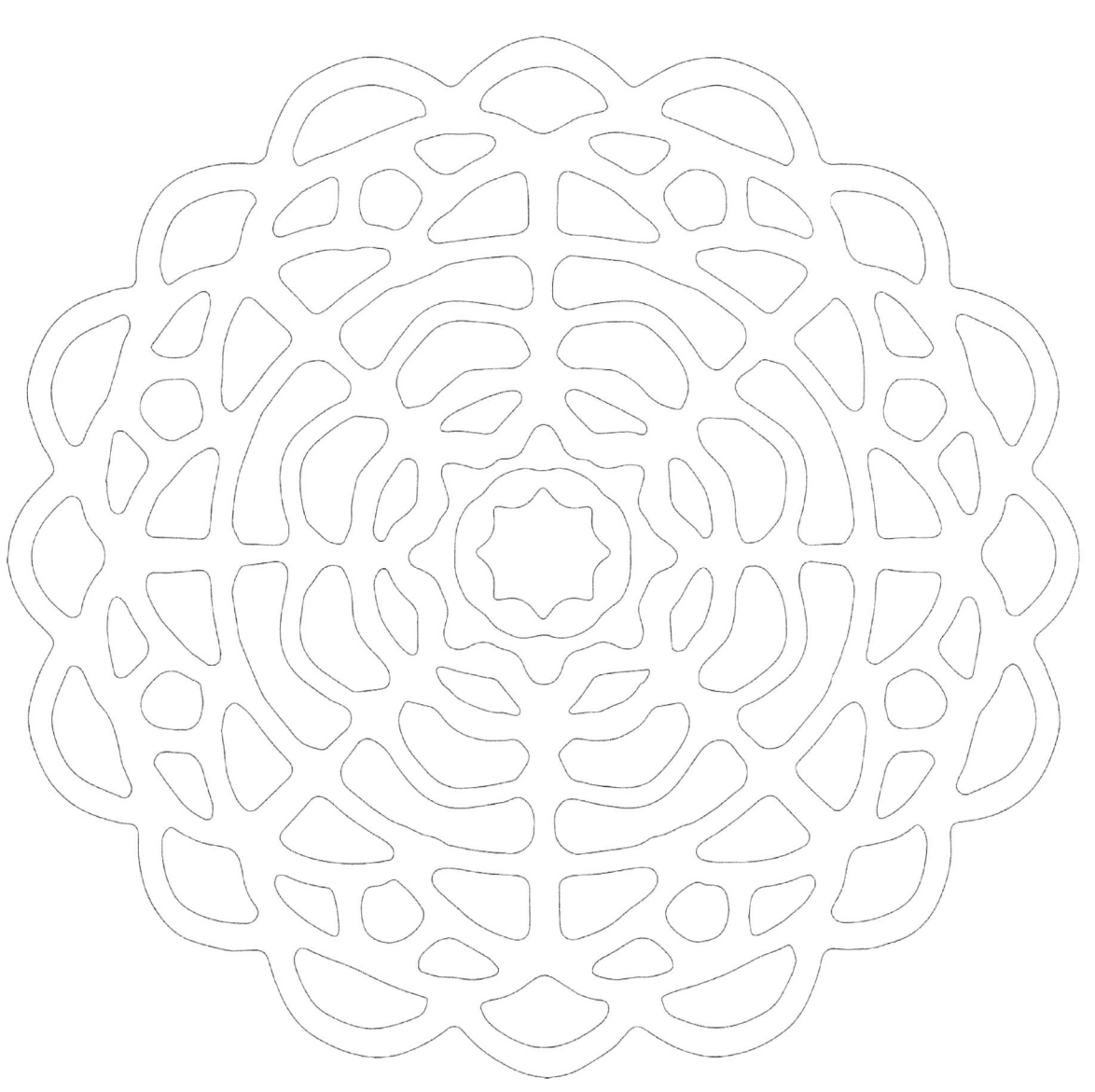

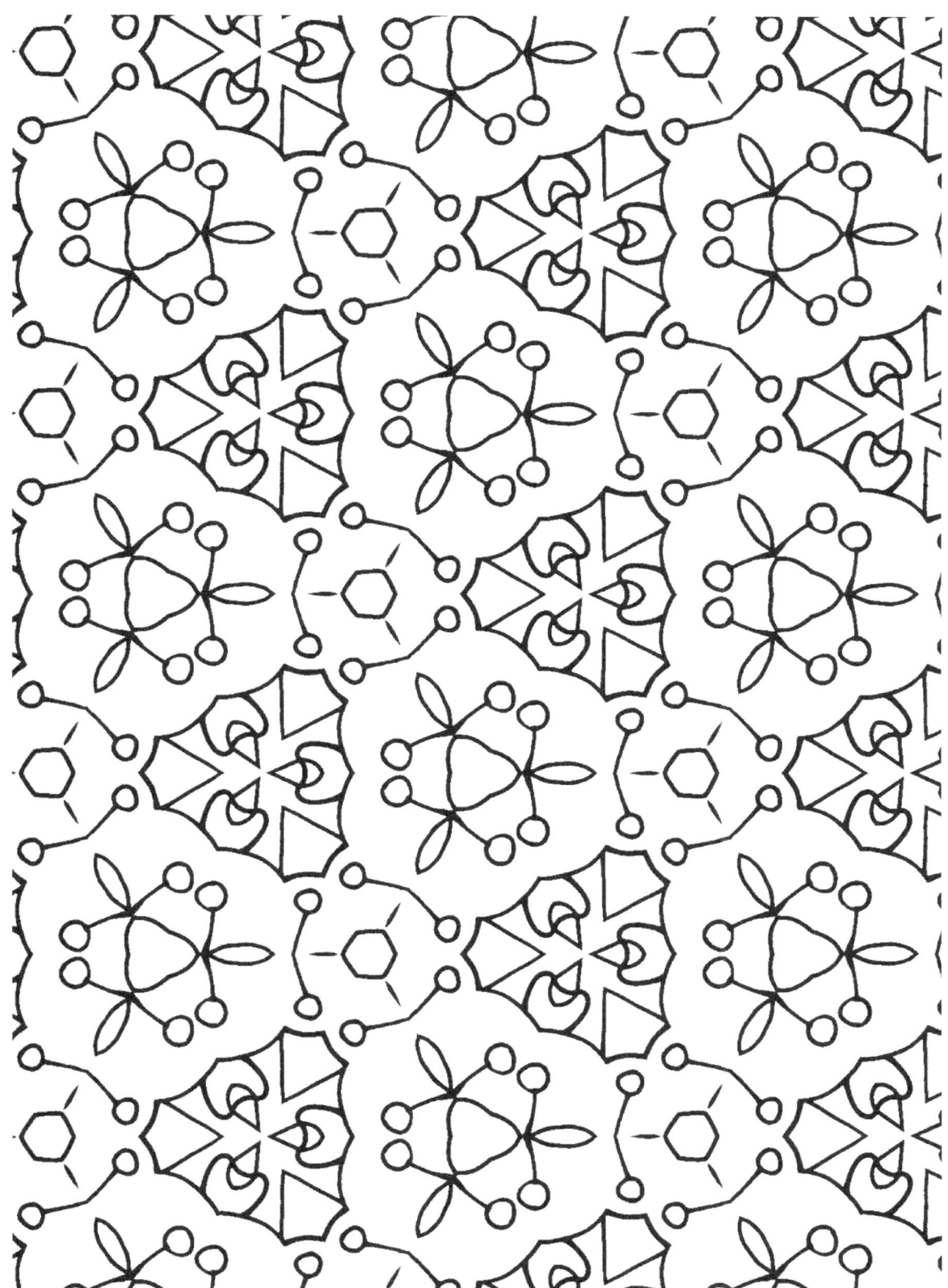

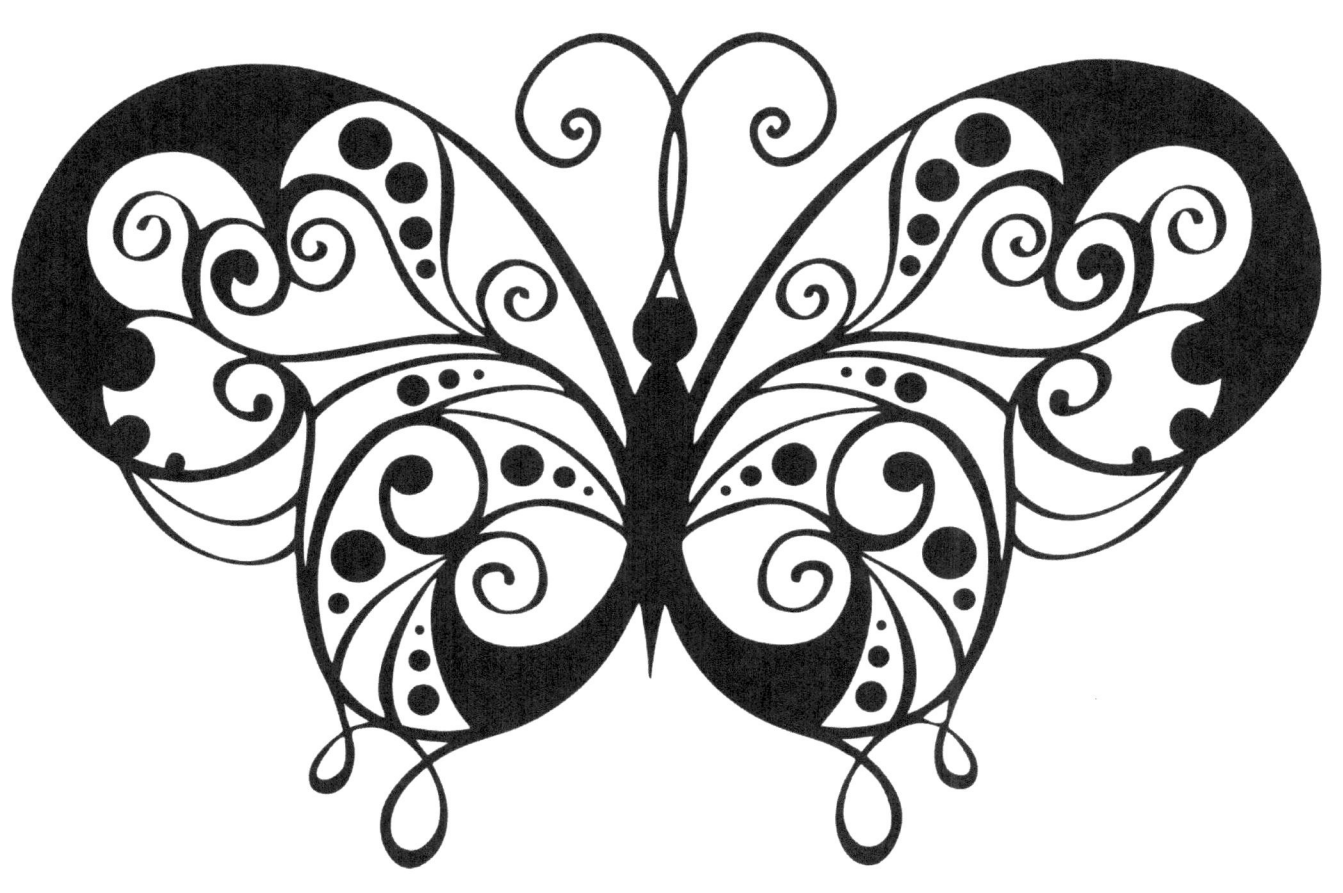

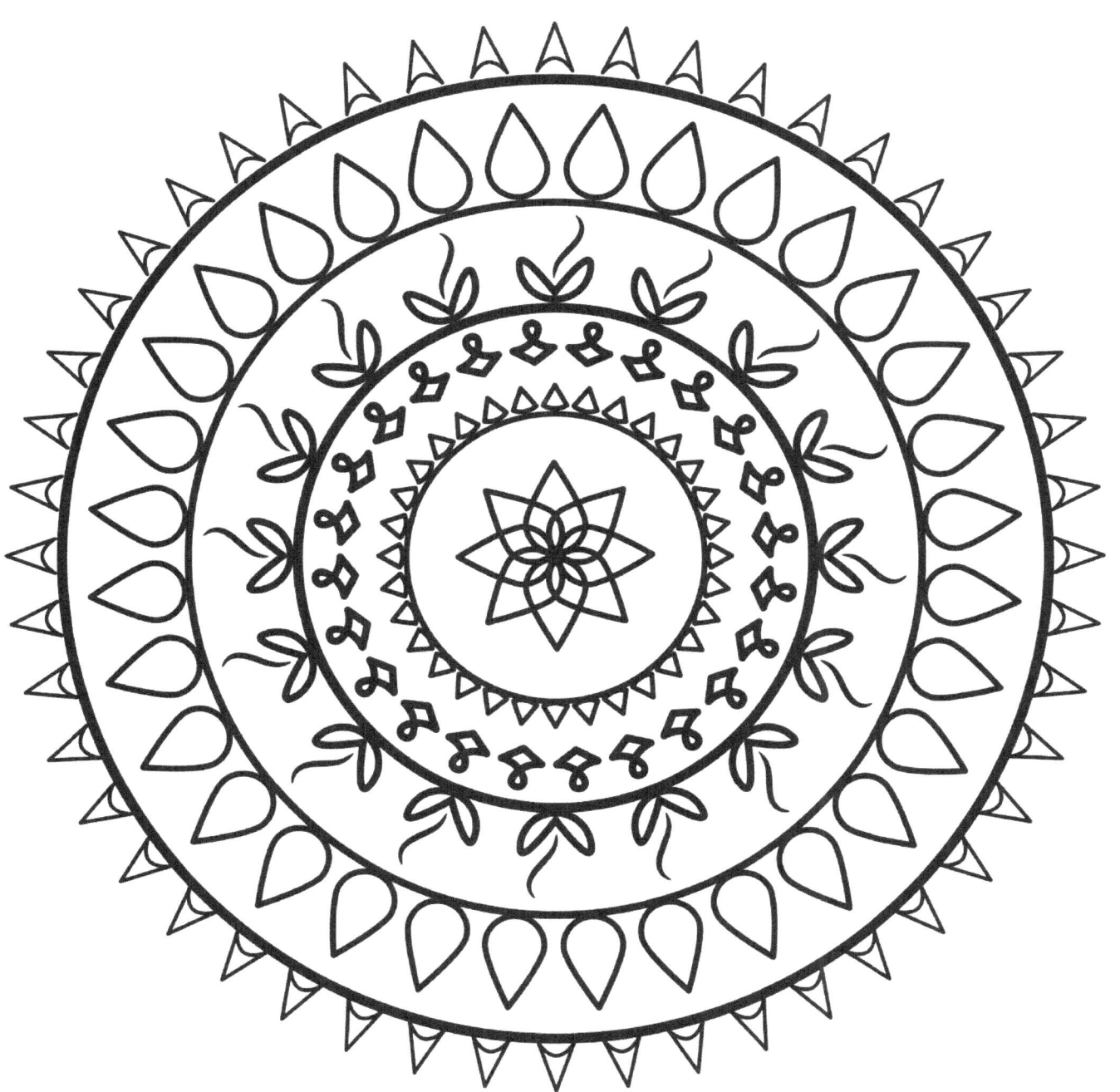

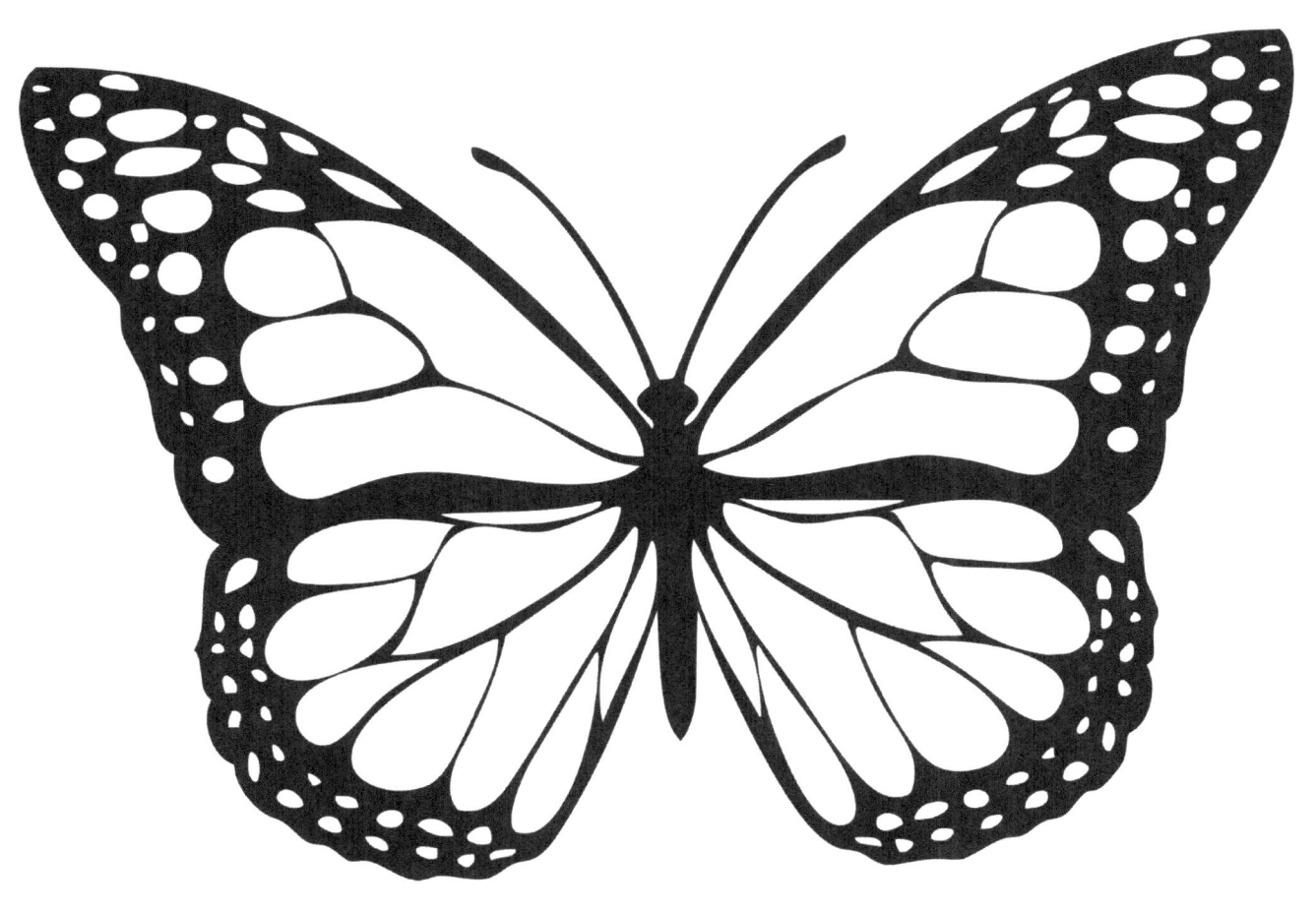

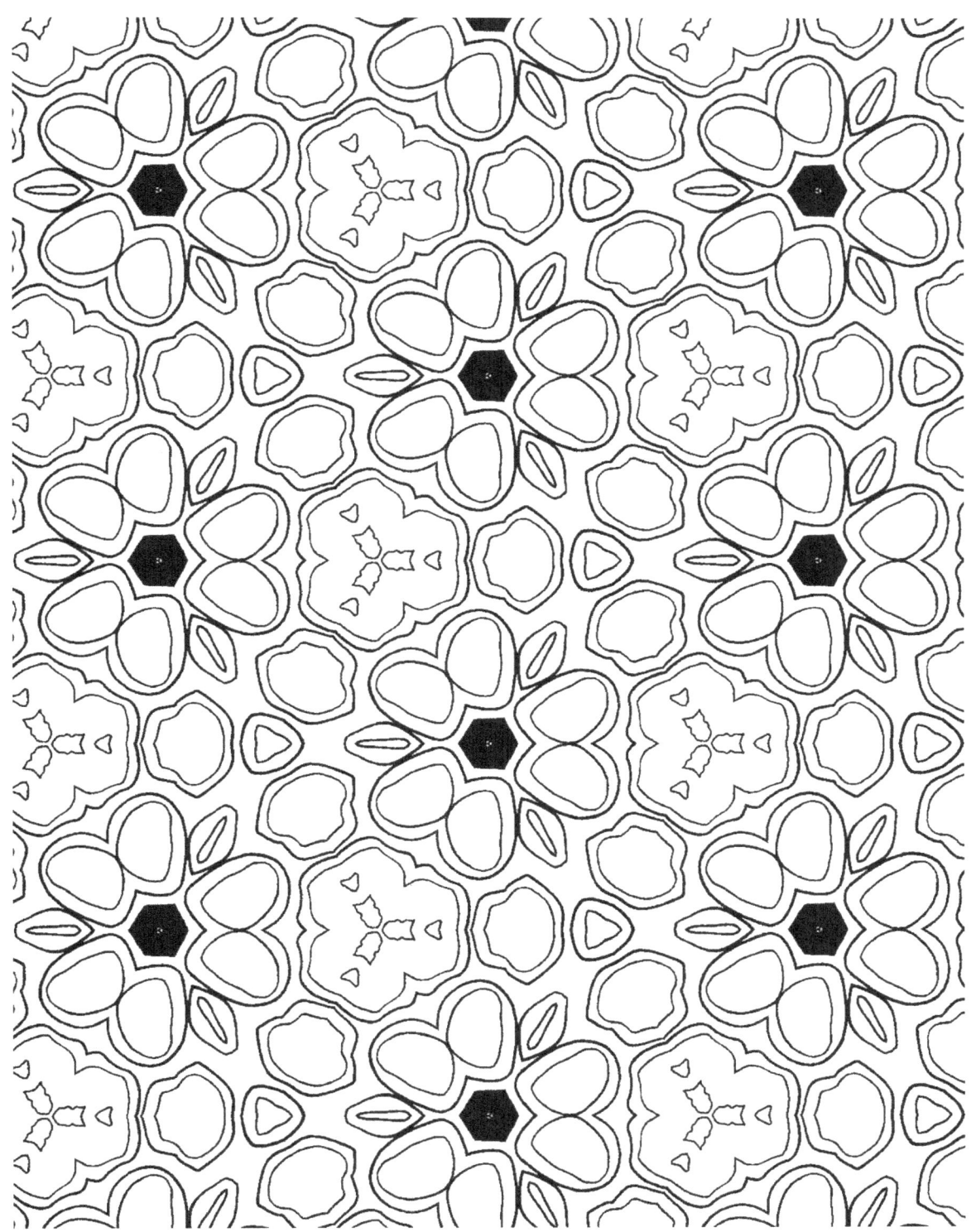

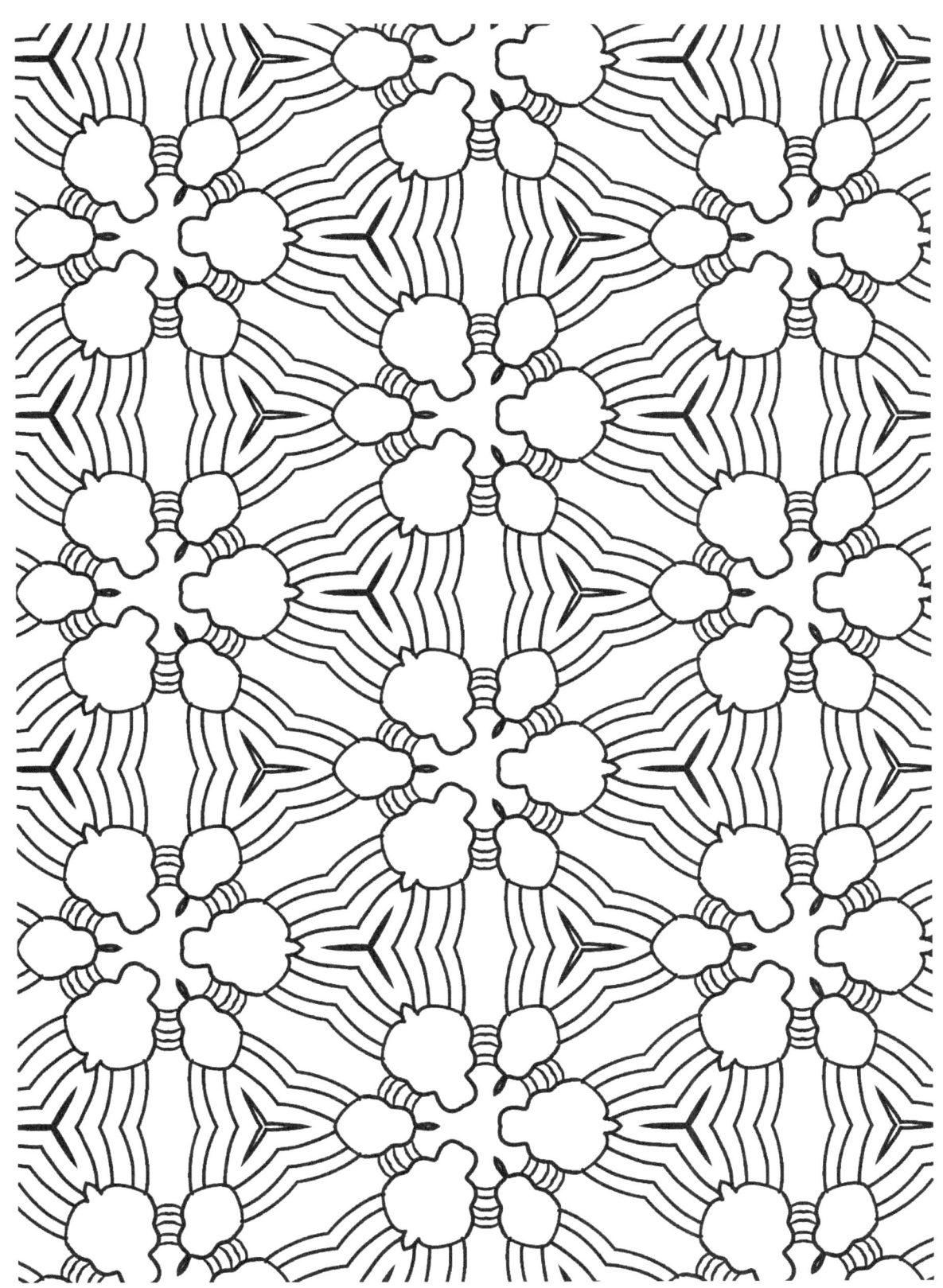

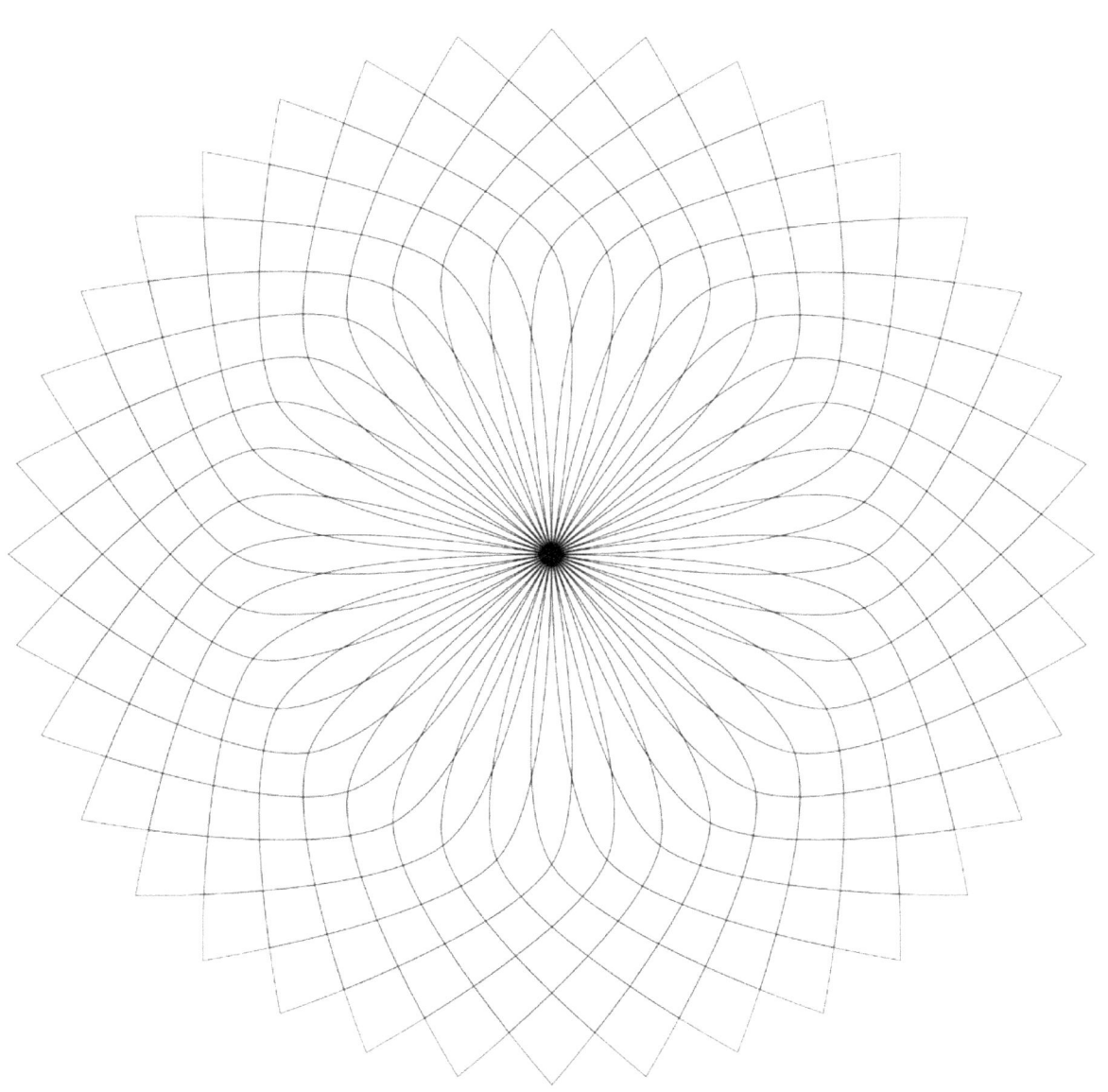

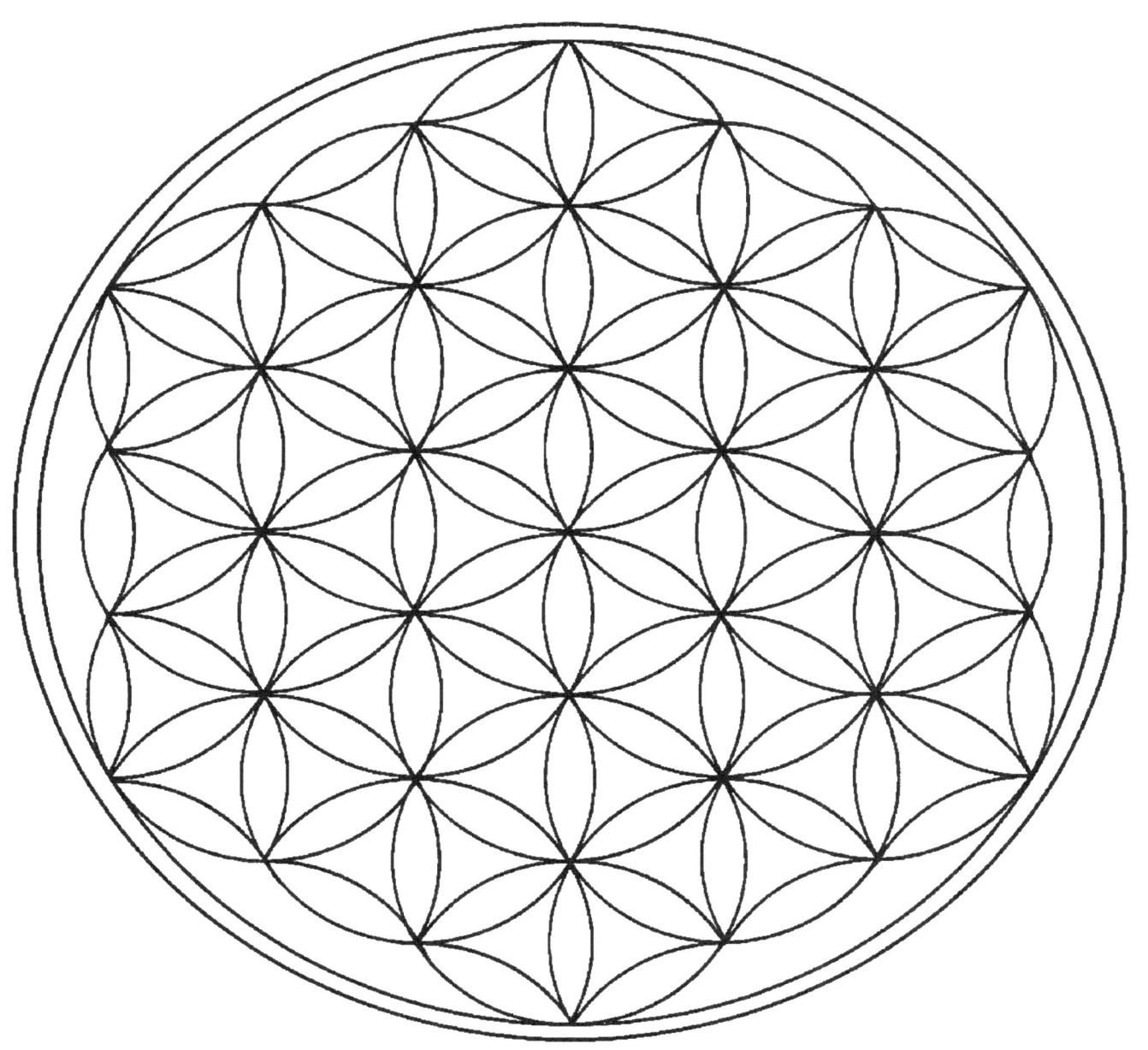

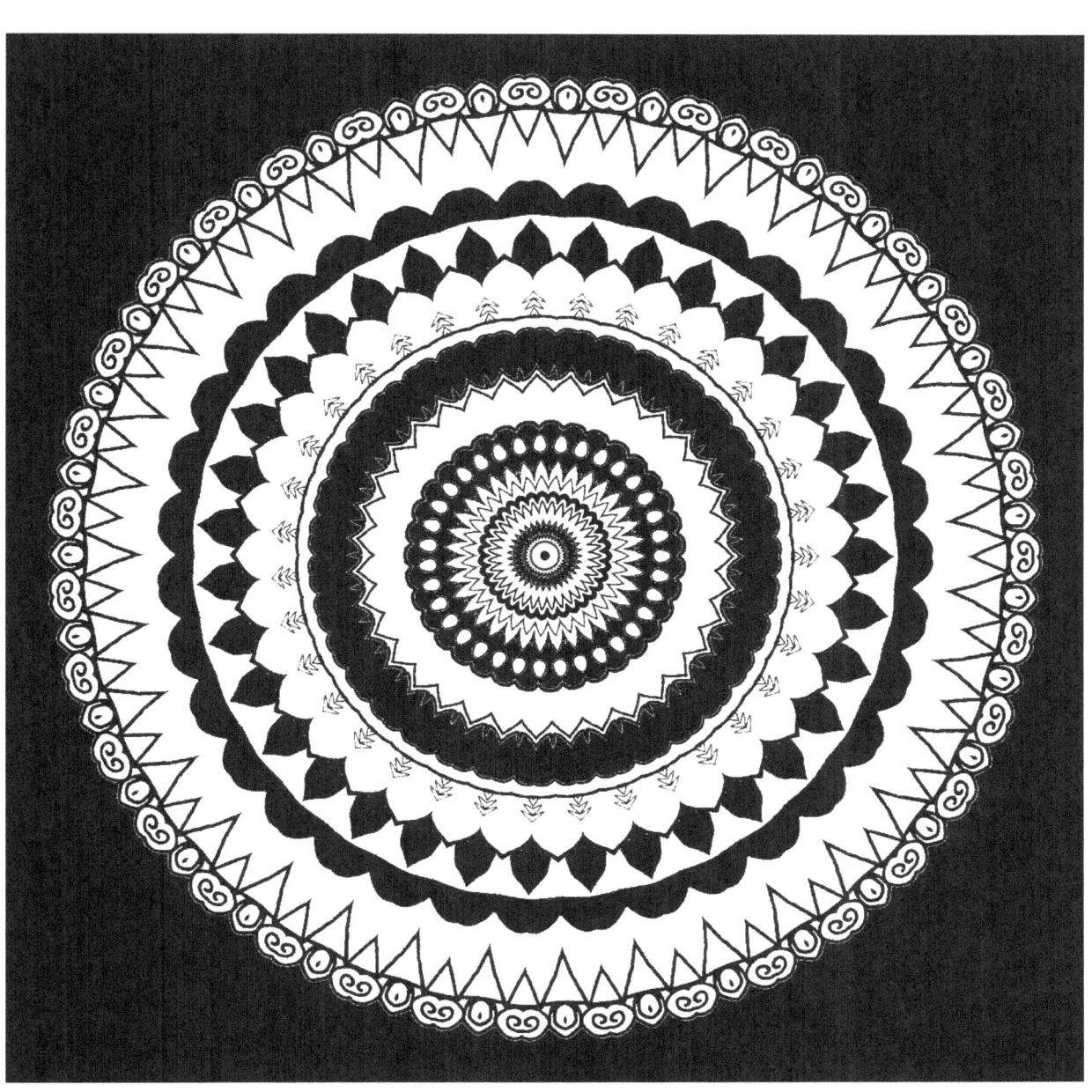

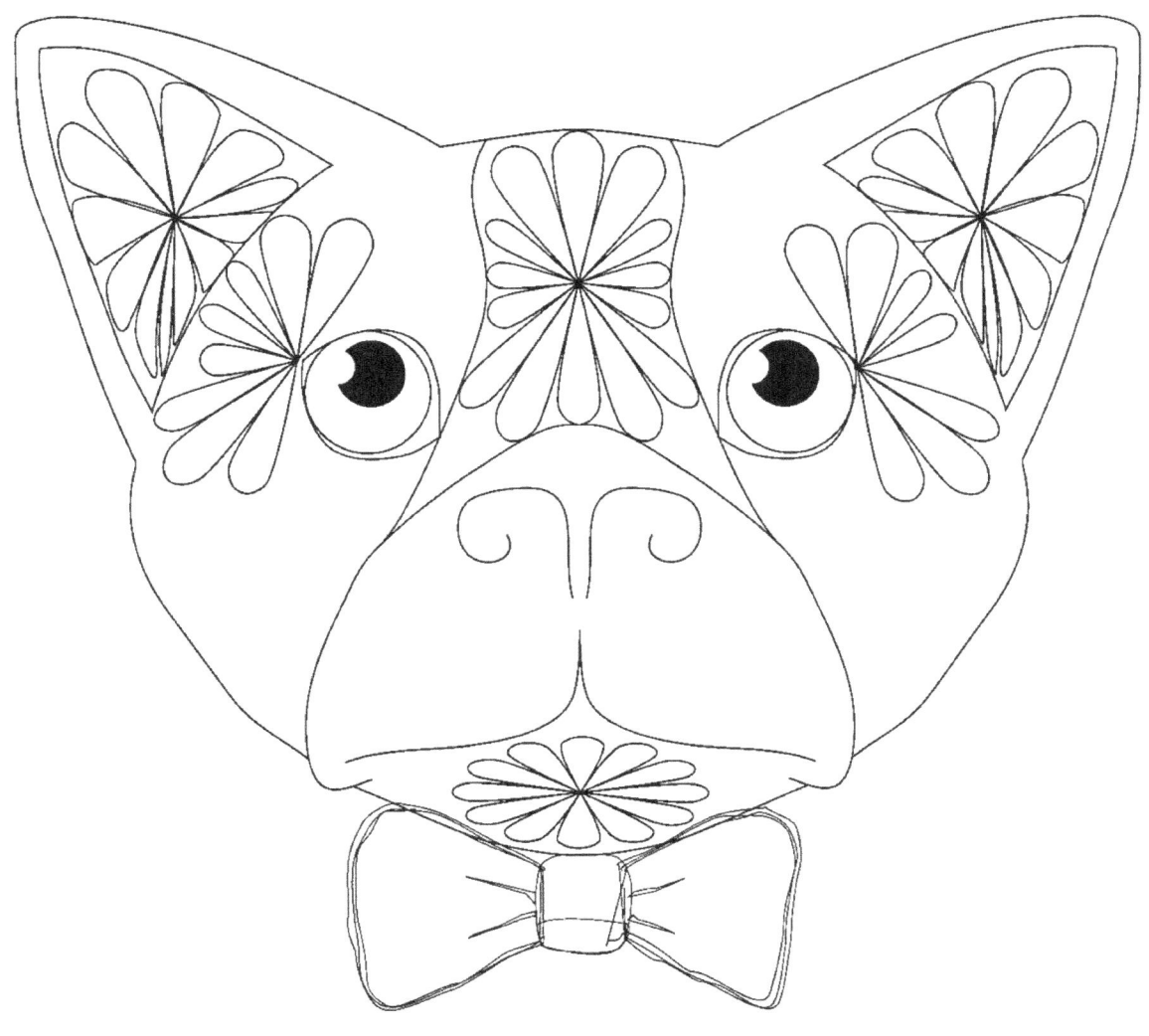

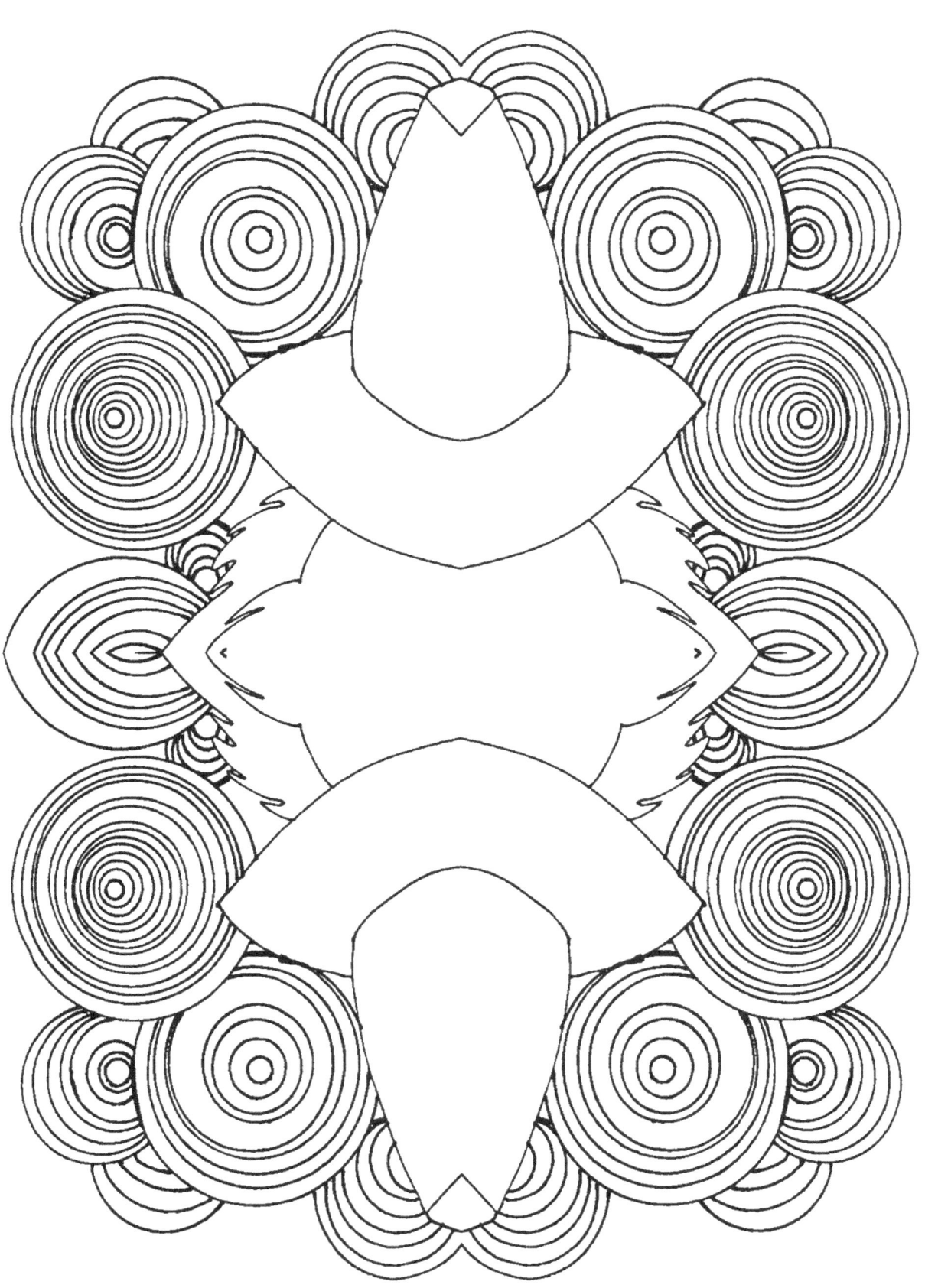

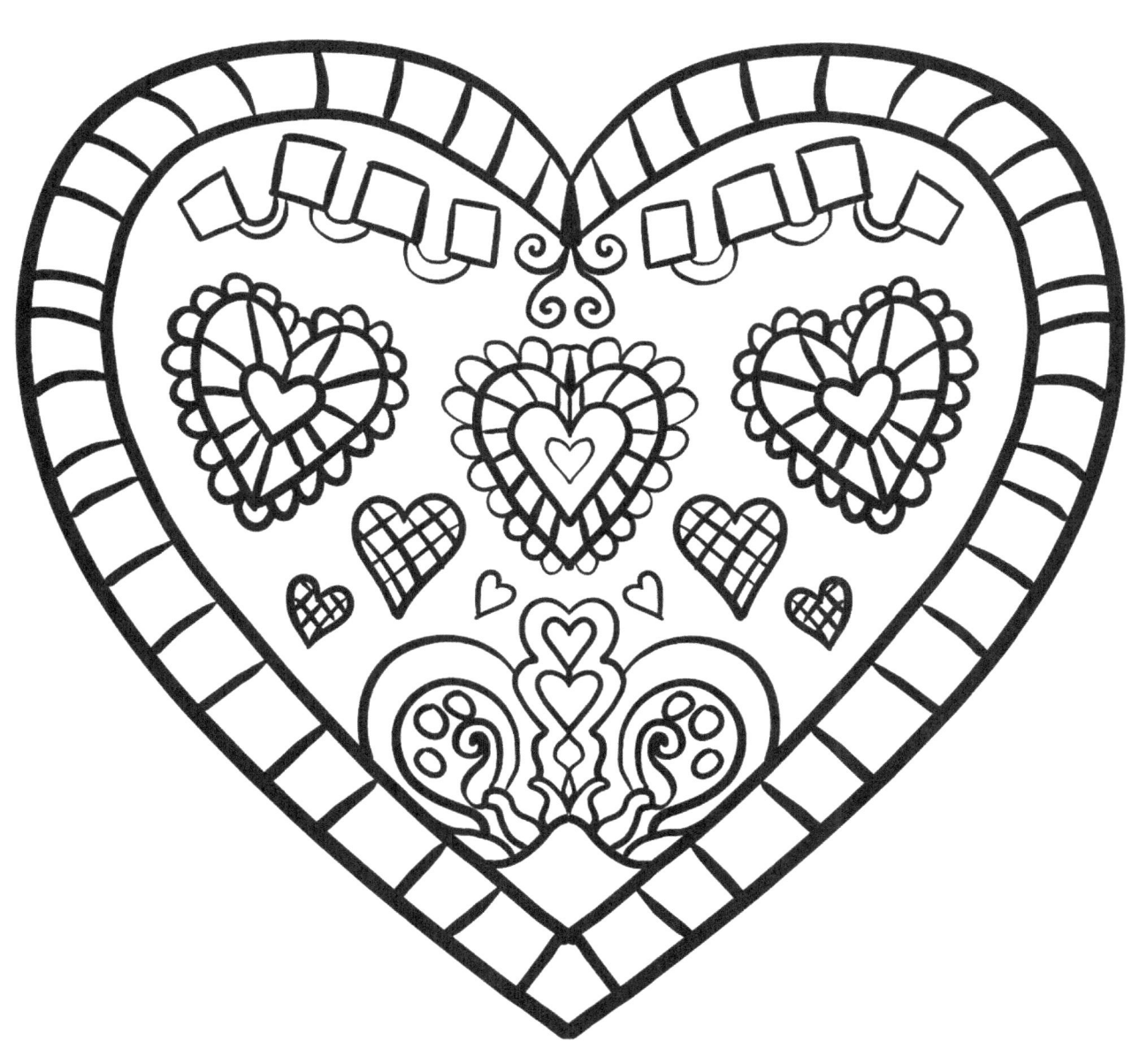

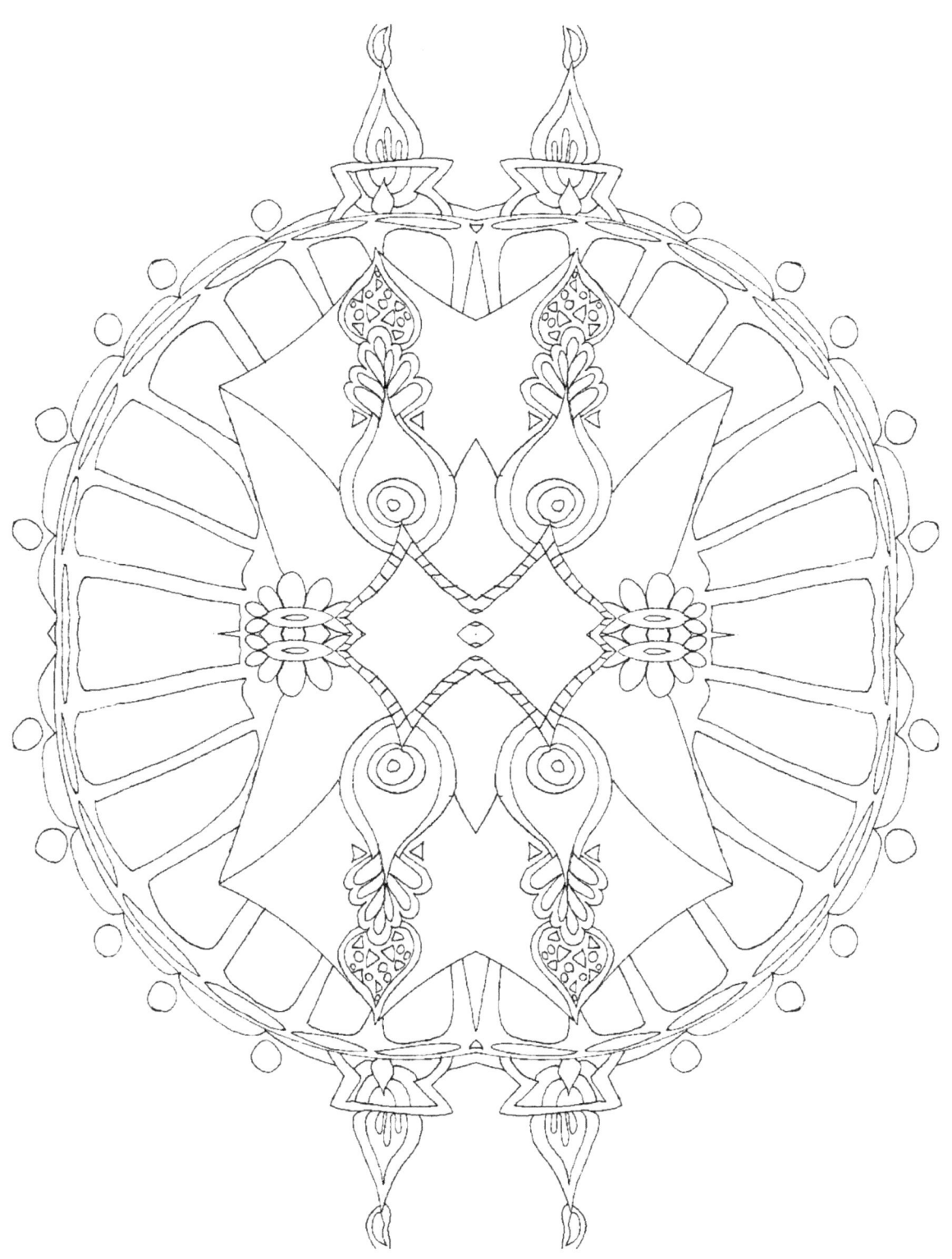

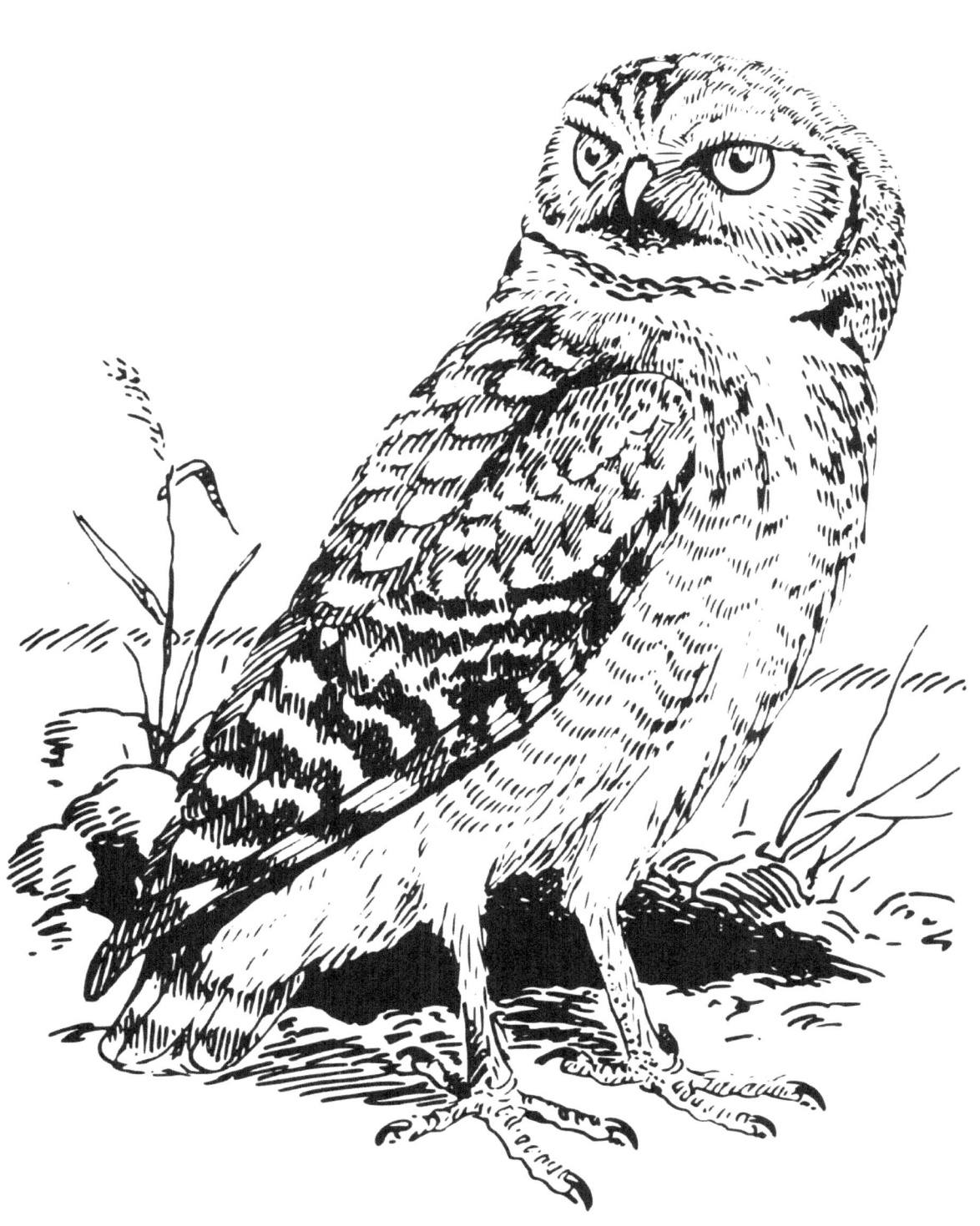

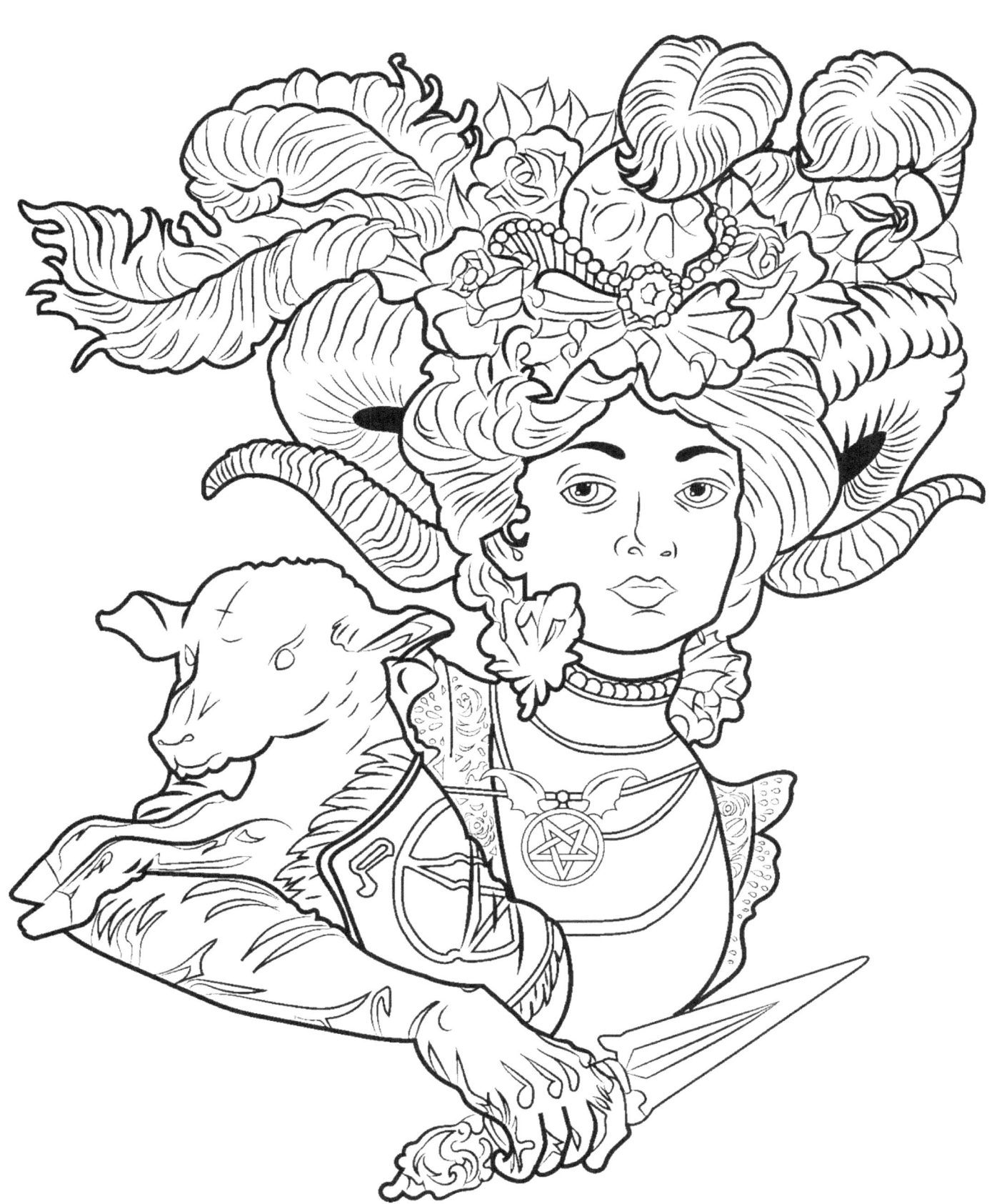

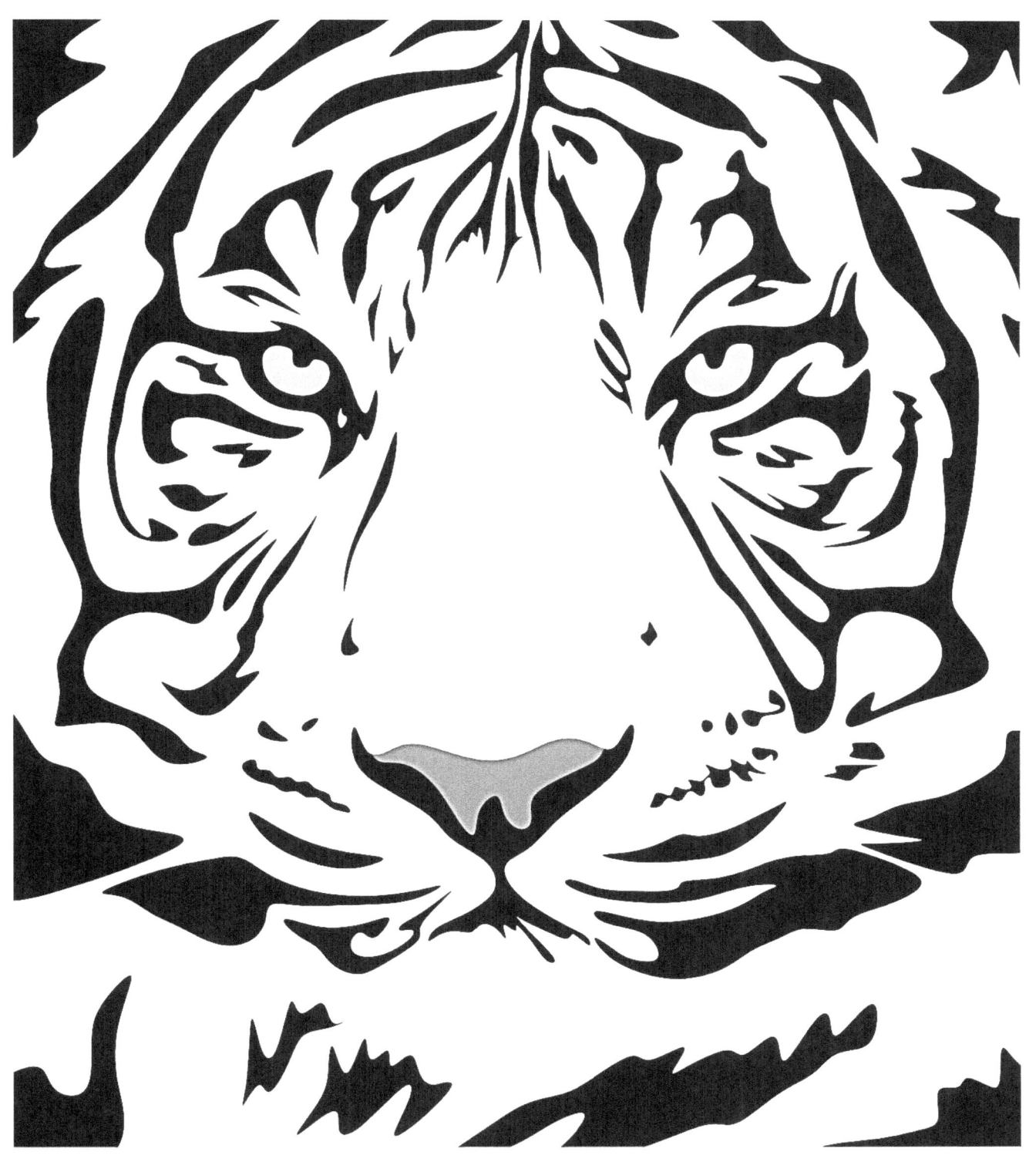

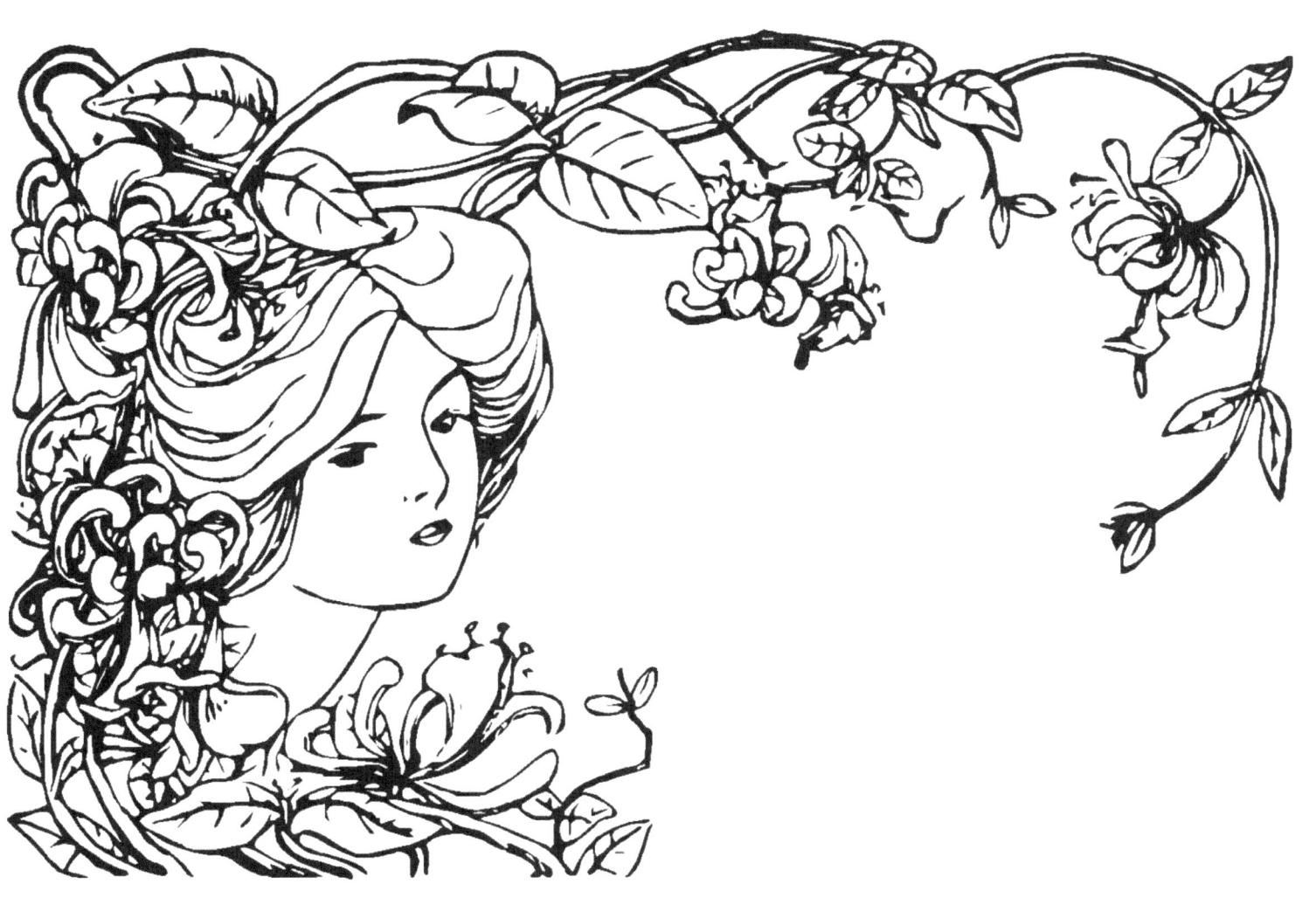

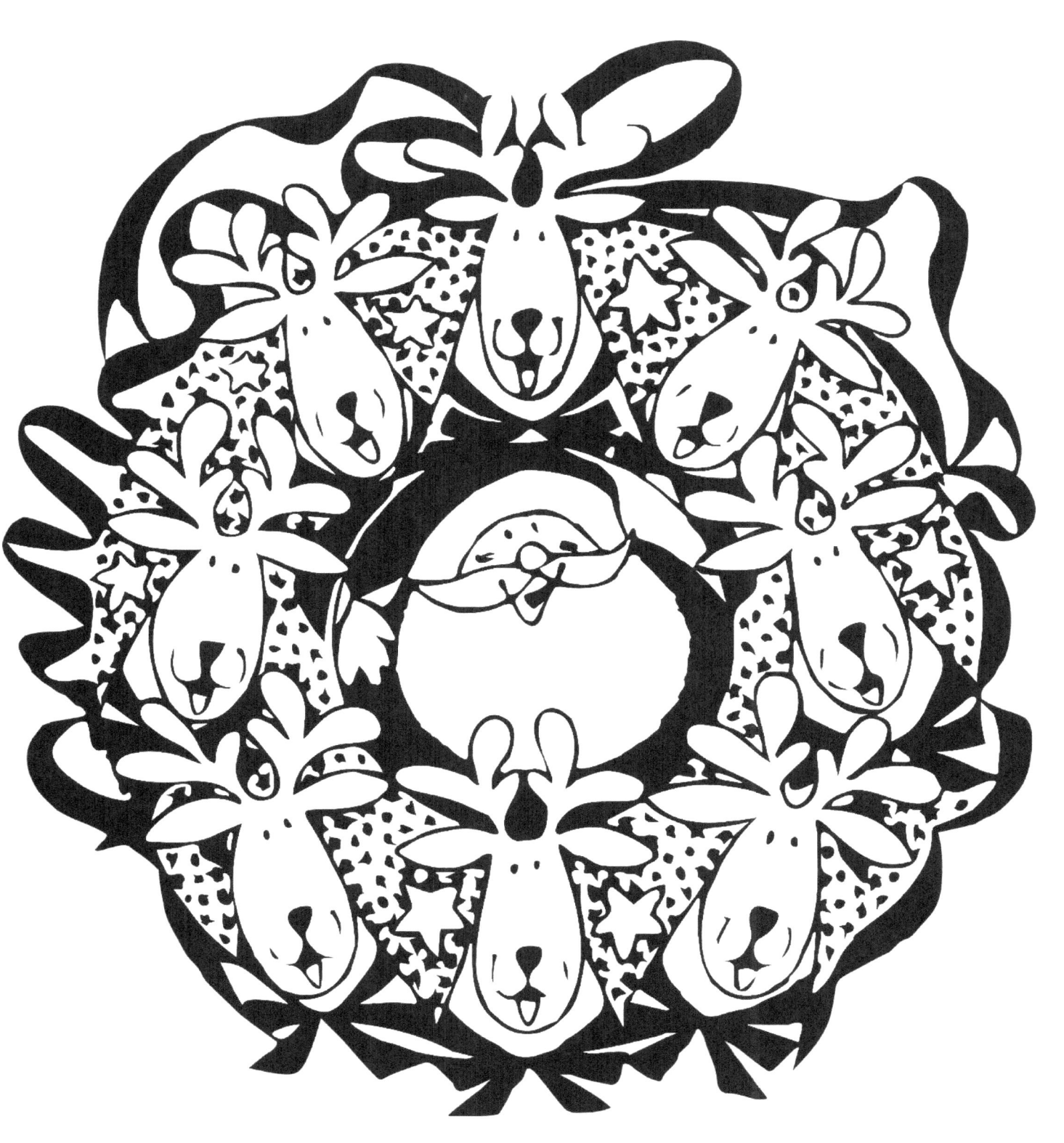

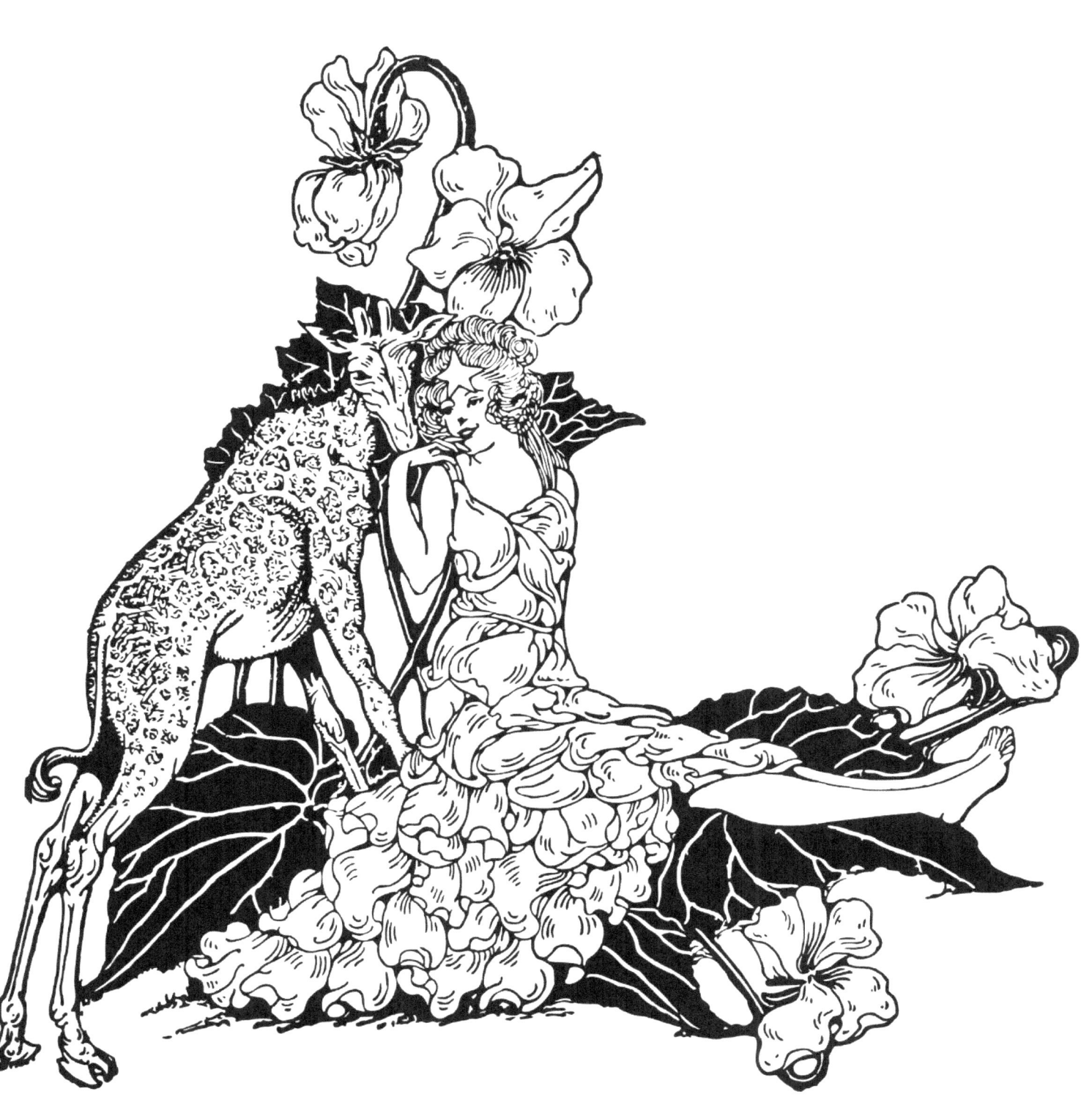

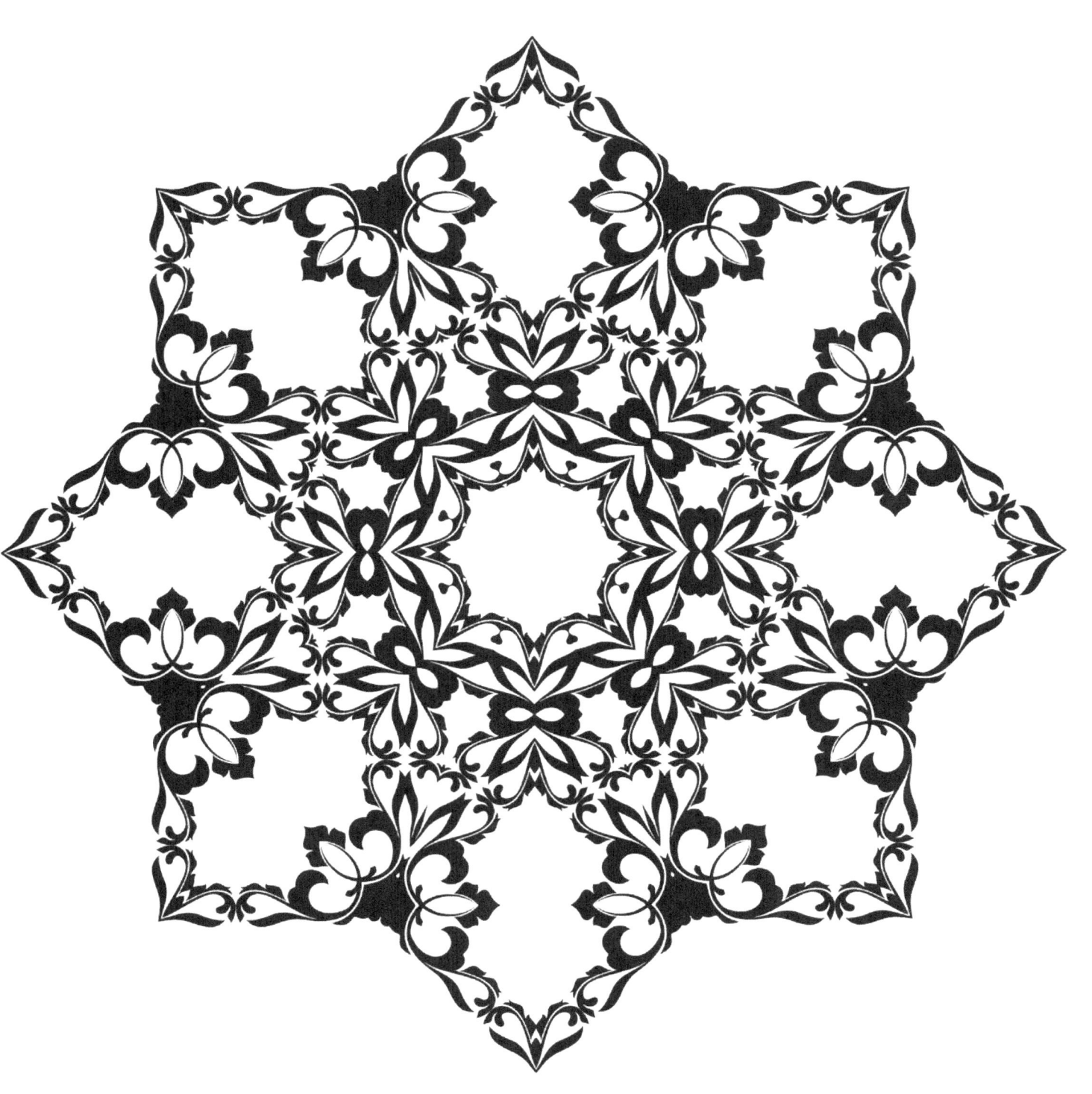

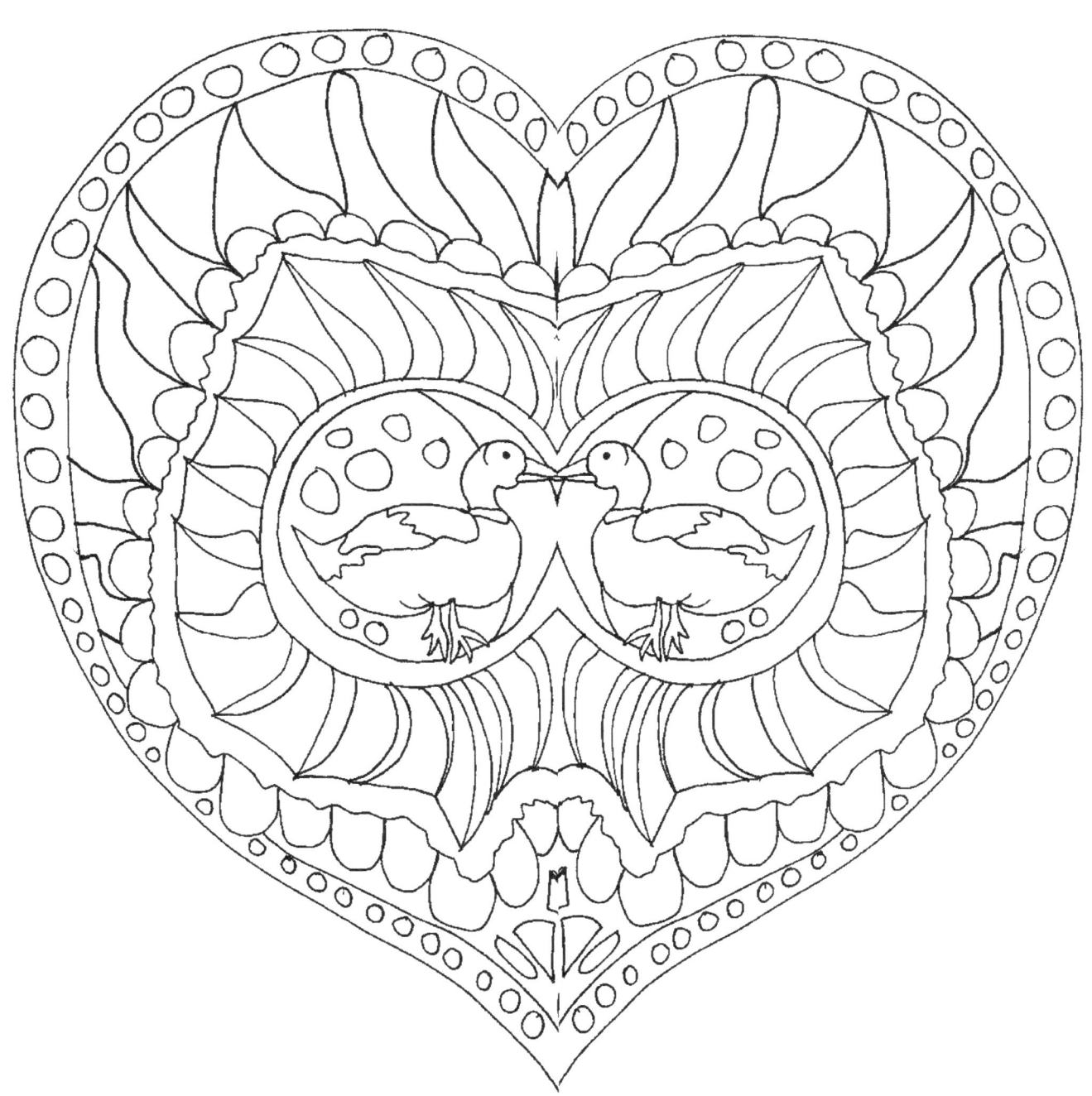

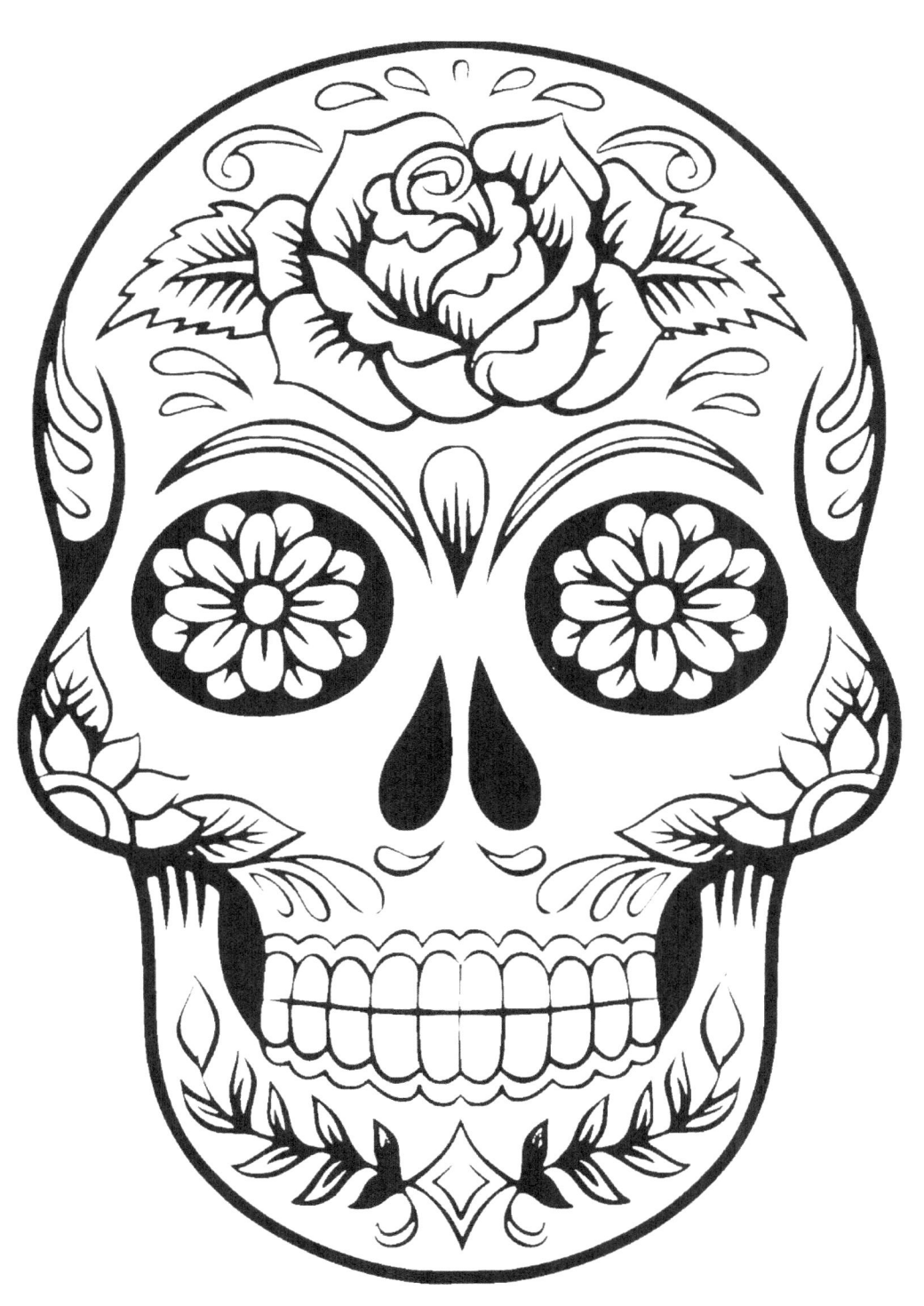

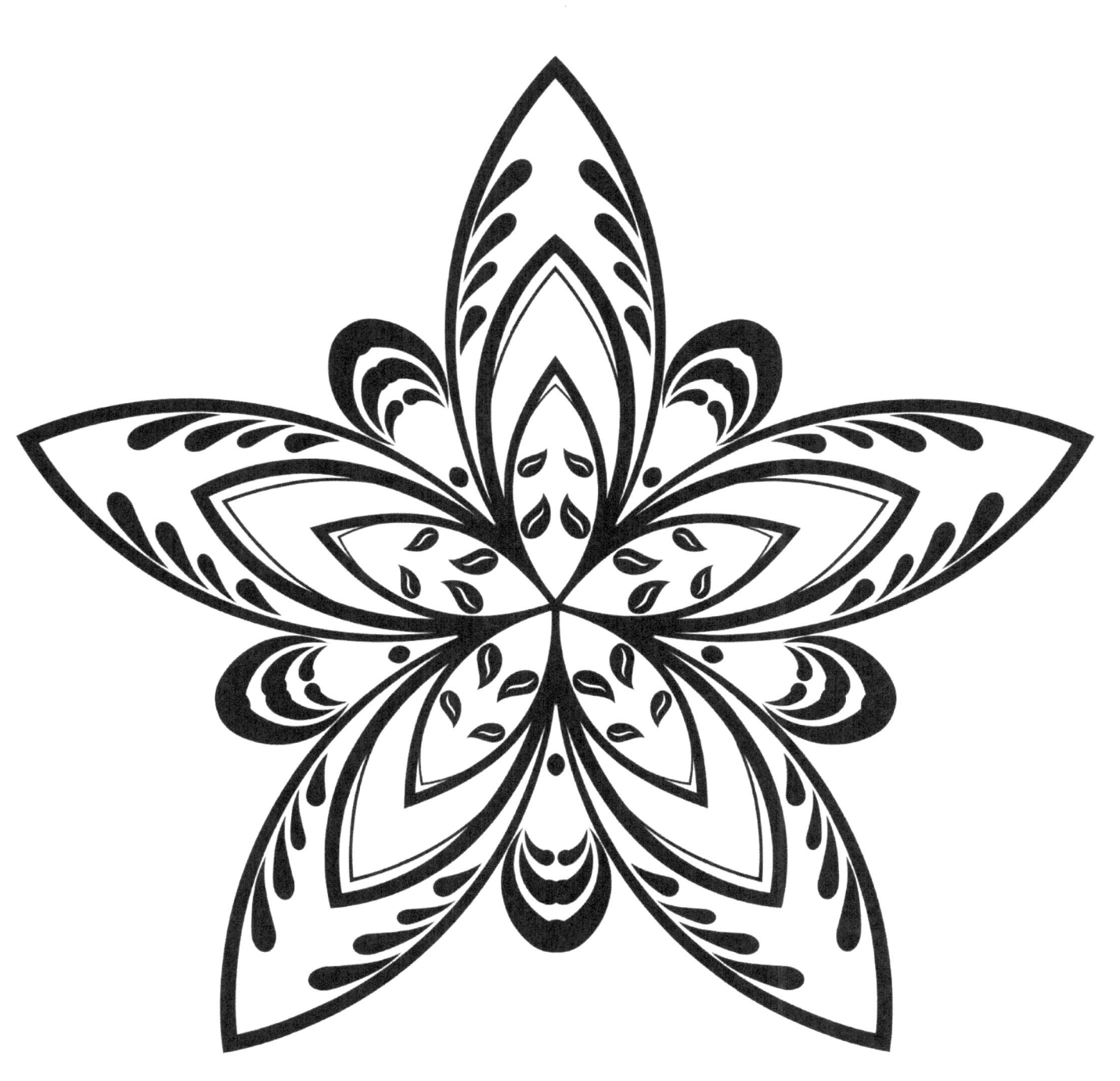

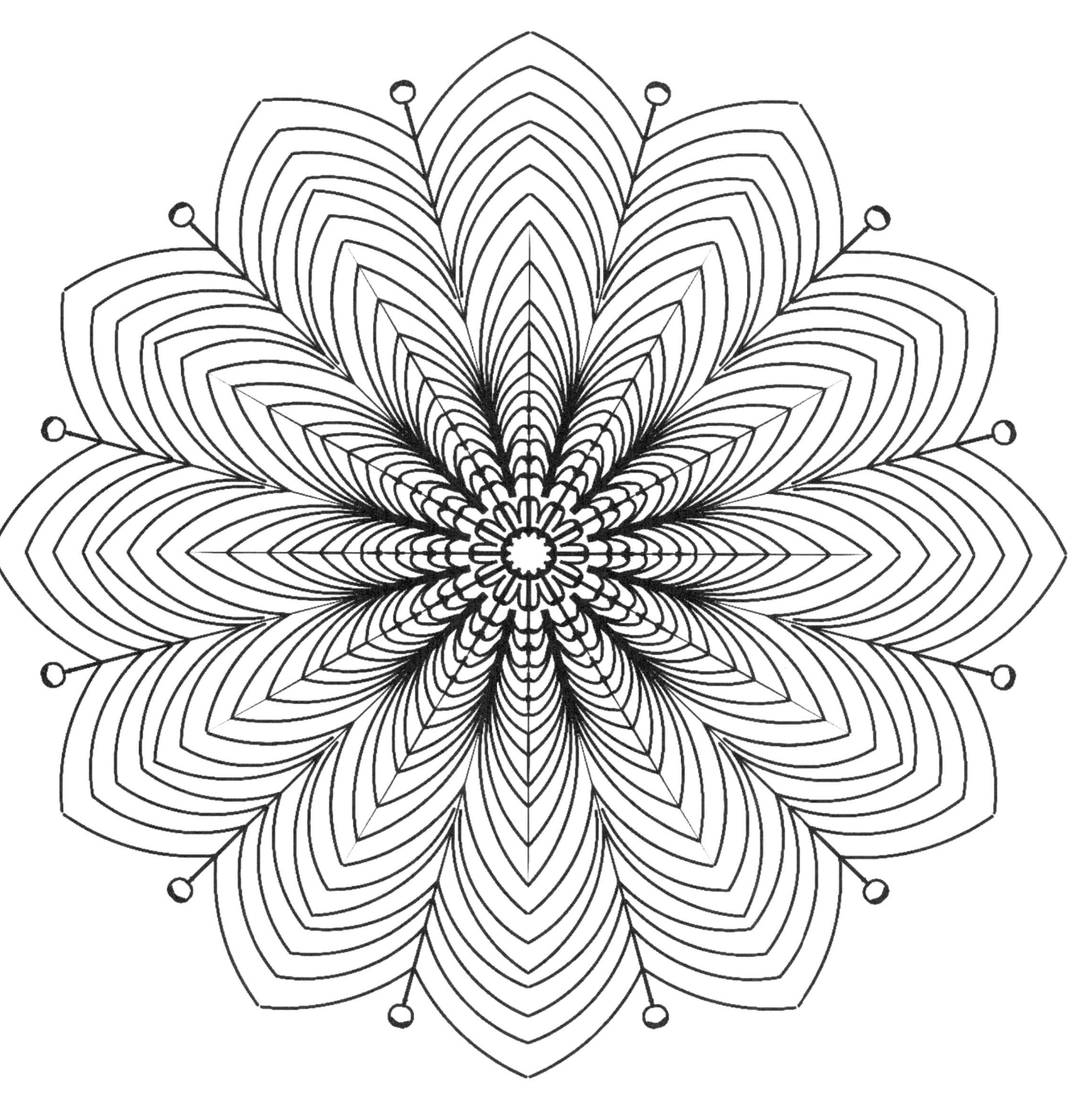

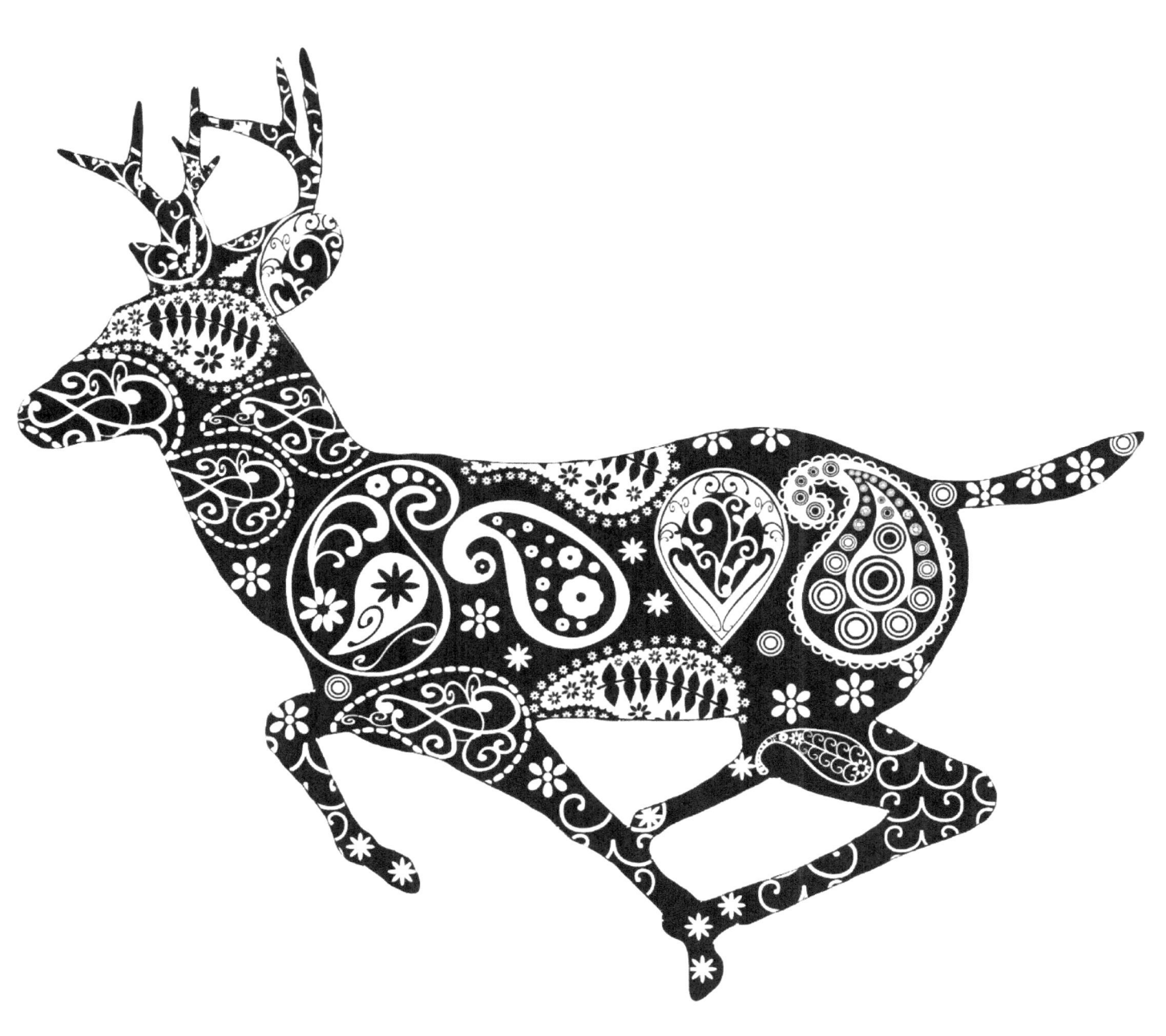

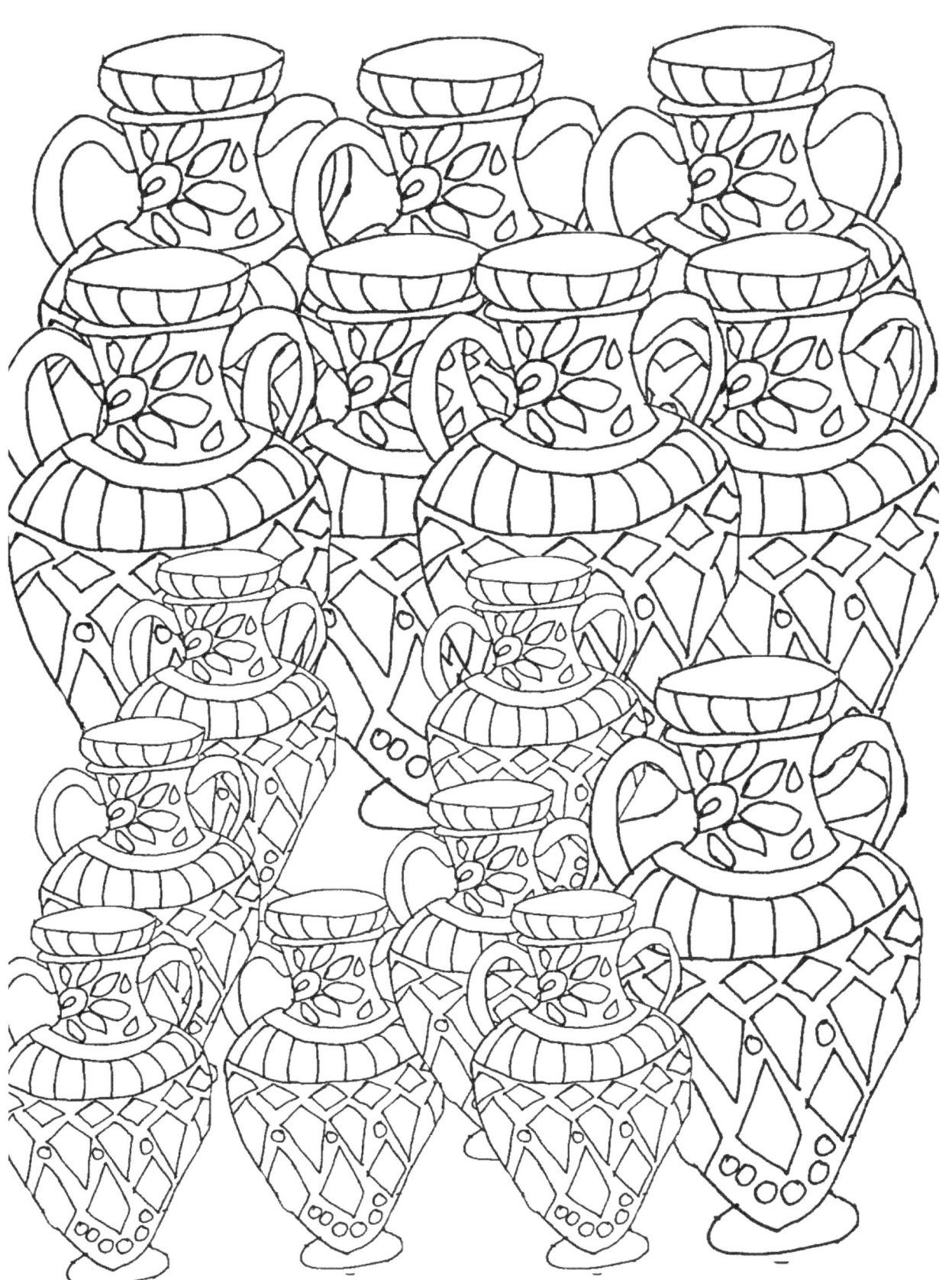

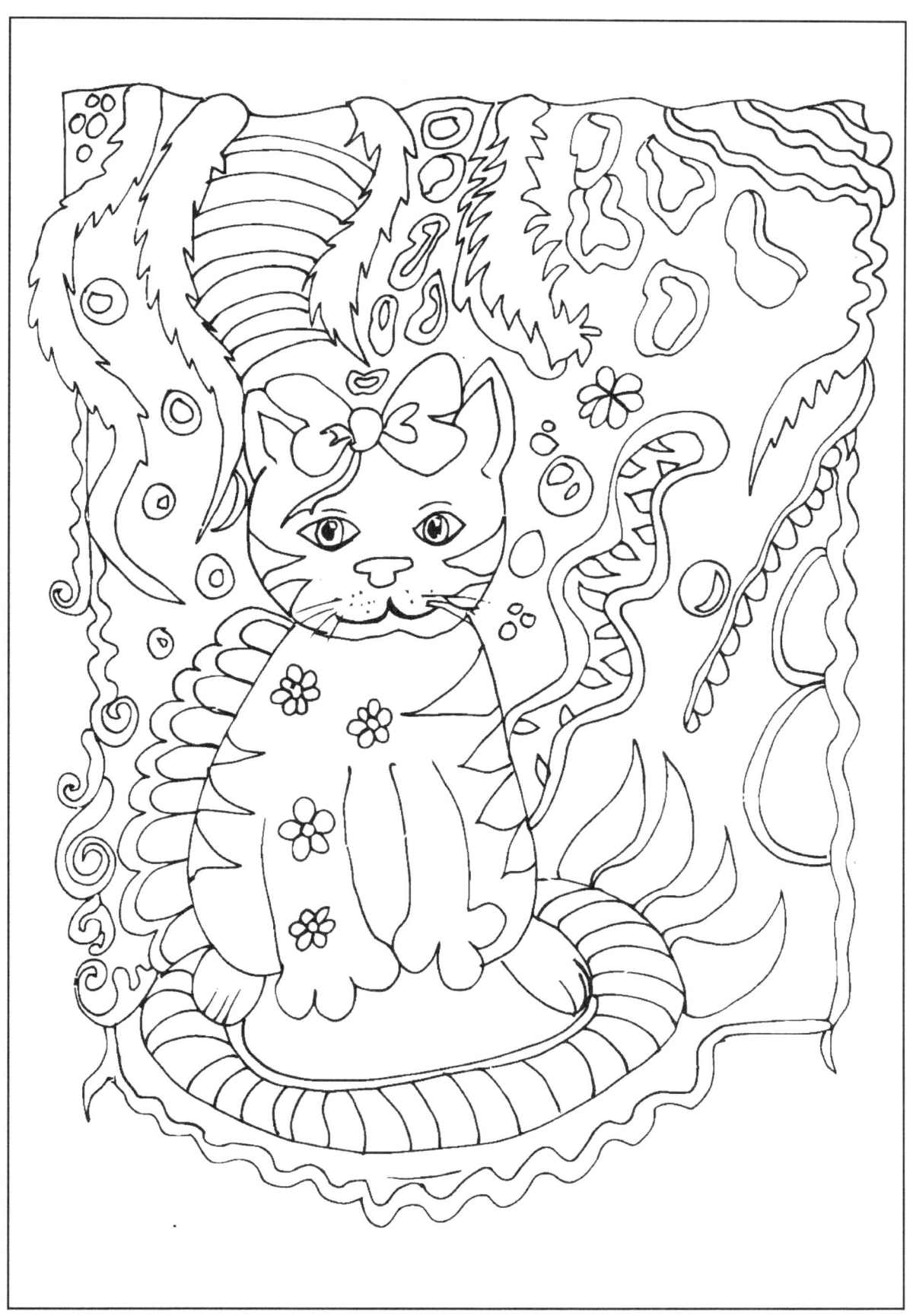

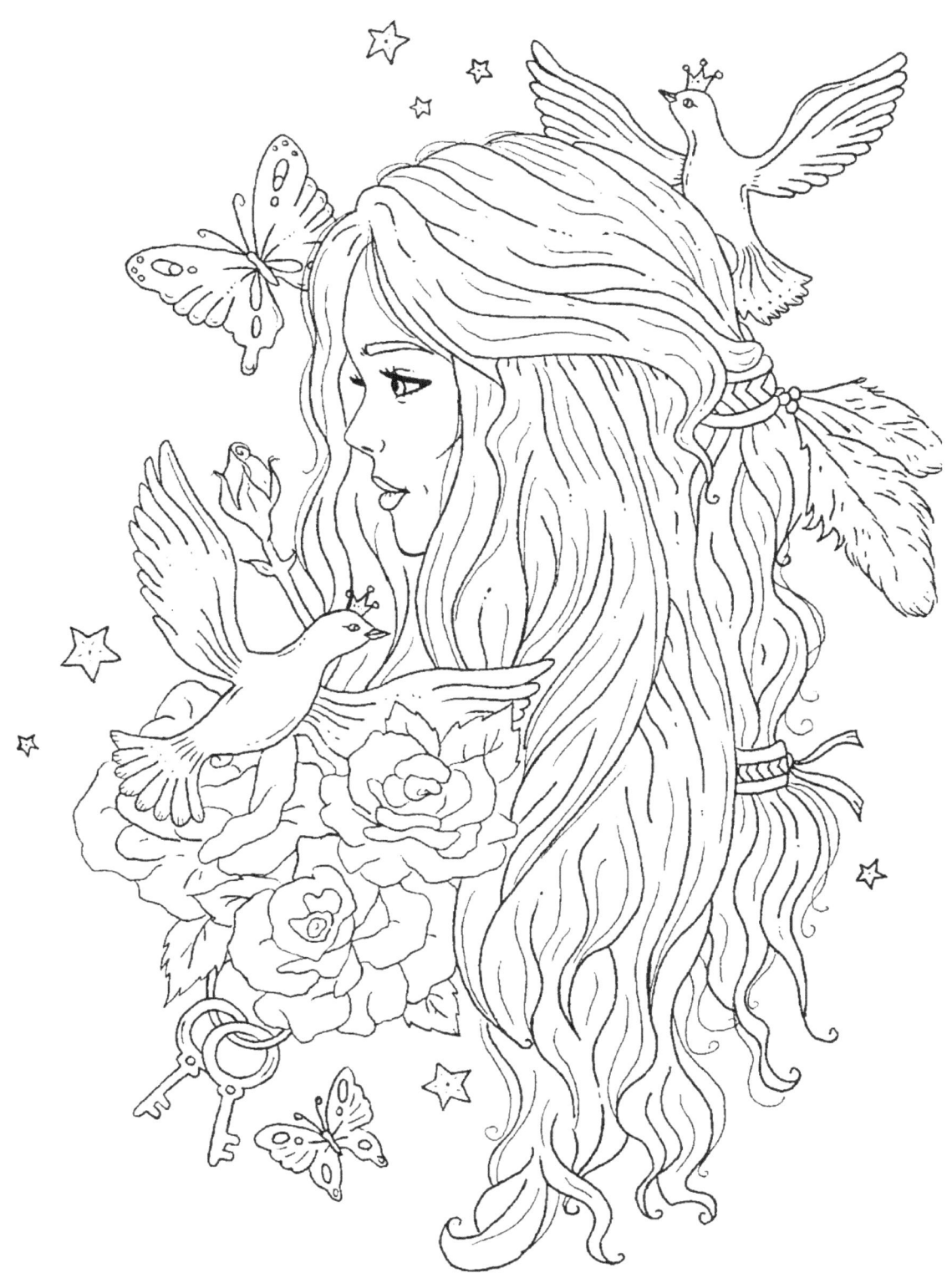

www.ingramcontent.com/pod-product-compliance
Lightning Source LLC
Chambersburg PA
CBHW060433220526
45465CB00008B/3126